Tosca

BLACK DOG OPERA LIBRARY

Tosca

GIACOMO PUCCINI

TEXT BY DANIEL S. BRINK

BLACK DOG
& LEVENTHAL
PUBLISHERS
NEW YORK

The enclosed compact discs © 1997 EMI Records Ltd.
Product of EMI-Capitol Music Special Markets, 1750 North Vine Street,
Los Angeles, California 90028.

Libretto reproduced by courtesy of Angel/EMI Classics.

Published by
Black Dog & Leventhal Publishers, Inc.
151 West 19th Street
New York, NY 10011

Distributed by
Workman Publishing Company
708 Broadway
New York, NY 10003

Series editor: Jessica MacMurray
Original Series Design by Alleycat Design, Inc.
Layout by Dutton & Sherman Design

Book manufactured in Canada

ISBN: 1-57912-048-2

h g f e d c b a

FOREWORD

Giacomo Puccini was one of the masters—he blended poignant love stories with violent revenge, heartbreaking music with intense poetry. *Tosca* is one of his greatest works and has become a vital part of the modern repertoire. Discover Tosca's fiery jealousy, Scarpia's abusive power and Cavaradossi's honorable devotion in this timeless classic of the operatic stage.

You will hear the entire opera on the two compact discs included on the inside front and back covers of this book. As you explore the book, you will discover the story behind the opera and its creation, the life of the composer, biographies of the principal singers and conductor, and the opera's text—or libretto—both in Italian and English. Expert commentary has been added to the libretto to aid in your appreciation and to highlight key moments in the score.

Enjoy this book and enjoy the music.

PHOTOGRAPHY CREDITS

About the Author

*D*aniel S. Brink is the author of three other titles in the Black Dog Oper a Library: *La Traviata, Madama Butterfly* and *Rigoletto.* He is also the Artistic Advisor and Principal Coach/Accompanist for the Colorado Opera Festival, Artistic Director for the Company Singers, a development program for young operatic hopefuls and Artistic Director/Conductor of the Colorado Springs Choral Society small ensemble, MOSIAC. Mr. Brink is a lecturer in Music and principal accompanist at The Colorado College, and has performed extensively in the United States and Europe. He is a highly regarded director, recitalist, teacher, adjudicator and writer.

GIACOMO PUCCINI
(1858-1924)

Tosca

Since its premiere in 1900, *Tosca* has proven to be one of Puccini's most enduring achievements—it has remained a mainstay of the repertoire of opera houses the world over. It is the fifth of his twelve operas and was written when the composer was riding the crest of the wave of his early success.

On December 22, 1858, Giacomo Puccini was born in Lucca, a city of about 30,000 people in Tuscany. He was the first son to be born to Michele Puccini and Albina-Magi Puccini—who were already the parents of six daughters. Five generations of Puccini men had studied music at the Naples Conservatory and served as Maestro di Capella Palatina at the local Cathedral of San Martino. The family had held this position since 1739 and it was assumed that Giacomo would be the heir apparent to this respected and demanding musical post. He would never take his expected place in the Cathedral, but his musical talents would endear him to a far broader public than that of any of his locally famous ancestors.

Sadly, when Giacomo was only five years old, his father suddenly died and his widow's brother, Fortunato Magi, was appointed to take over the musical directorship at the cathedral until Giacomo's age and training allowed him to assume his father's position. Magi also took over as Giacomo's first music teacher—unfortunately, it was a very poor match. Giacomo responded poorly to his uncle's dictatorial style and Magi believed him to be without sufficient talent to pursue music as a career. His uncle wasn't the only teacher to find fault in the young man's commitment to study—one of his teachers once complained that the only thing he accomplished in school was wear and tear on the seat of his pants.

Regardless, the young Puccini had an irrepressible ally in his mother, whose unfailing belief in him would prove to support and direct his steps throughout his formation and early career. He graduated from the local seminary school—where he had repeated his final year due to poor performance—and his mother immediately enrolled him in Lucca's music conservatory, the Pacini Institute. Here, Puccini encountered his first musical kindred spirit: Carlo Angeloni, a professor who had studied with Michele Puccini and whose operas and choral works were highly respected in the region. Angeloni was teacher, mentor and friend to young Giacomo, introducing him to the wonders of Verdi's operas in the classroom and sharing his student's passion for hunting in the countryside outside of town. The familial fascination with music was at last being awakened in the young man.

As his skills advanced, Puccini began contributing to the support of his mother's household by playing the organ in various area churches. It is recounted that he would steal an occasional organ pipe, sell it for scrap metal and use the funds to support his newly acquired passion for cigarettes, a habit which

MARIA CALLAS (TOSCA) AND TITO GOBBI (SCARPIA) AT COVENT GARDEN, 1964

would eventually cause his death of throat cancer in 1924. Even this petty larceny is said to have contributed to his development, since he was forced to avoid the notes whose pipes were missing, which led to some unaccustomed creativity in his harmonic progressions. He also stretched his professional wings playing in a local dance orchestra. At sixteen, he received the first prize in organ performance at the Institute.

The following year, Puccini encountered his first fully professional opera production. He had certainly seen small touring companies growing up and there was an annual festival at which an opera was produced mainly with local talent. But this was different. Giacomo and two friends walked seven hours to Pisa to see a production of Verdi's *Aida* at the Teatro Nuovo (now the Teatro Verdi). They had no money for tickets, so they hid high in the house's gallery for three hours awaiting the performance. *Aida,* the work of the aging "King of Italian Opera" had taken the world by storm since its premiere in Cairo five years earlier. The effect was not lost on the young composer—Puccini later wrote, "When I heard *Aida* in Pisa, I felt that a musical window had opened for me."

While Puccini could not help but revere the man whose genius had formed and sustained 19th century Italian Opera, his own style would prove to have more in common with that of Richard Wagner, with whom Verdi had been unfavorably compared throughout his career. With Puccini's generation, Italian Opera abandoned the tradition of building an opera score out of a series of set pieces and began "through-composing" a score using short melodic ideas representing specific characters, situations and emotions to unify the work and propel the action. These short musical ideas had been dubbed "leitmotifs" by Wagner and Puccini's skill in creating and molding these ideas in his own works was unsurpassed by any of his contemporaries.

By the time Puccini graduated from the Institute, he had so distinguished himself that it was clear his talent would take him beyond the provincial confines of a musical career in his hometown. His mother set about to send him to study at the Milan Conservatory, the most highly respected music school in Italy and the center of Italian artistic and operatic life at the time. Her determination led her to petition the queen for assistance, which was granted, but was still insufficient to sustain her son in Milan. So she turned to her late husband's cousin, Dr. Nicolai Ceru, who generously agreed to provide the remaining funds necessary to send her son for further study. Her steadfast love and faith secured him a place at the conservatory. In 1881, at the age of twenty-two, Giacomo arrived in Milan. He was well past the normal age for admittance to the Conservatory, but he performed so well on his entrance exams that he was admitted nonetheless. Again, he found a sympathetic mentor: Amilcare Ponchielli, whose opera *La Gioconda* defined the direction for post-Verdian Italian opera and is still performed regularly today. While he thrived artistically, Puccini's personal life was fraught with financial hardship, although the experience of poverty would prove to inform his depiction of the starving artists in his famous *La Boheme* in years to come. In June of 1883, he passed his final exams with flying colors. He had only to complete his final composition project. He chose to write an orchestral work, entitled Cappricio Sinfonico, which afforded him critical acclaim at it's premiere in July of 1883 and he graduated from the Conservatory having won the Bronze Medal, the school's highest honor.

Ponchielli had long encouraged Puccini to try his hand at opera and upon his graduation even secured a libretto for his talented student from a young poet named Ferdinando Fontana. This first effort, entitled *Le Villi,* based on a

LA SCALA, MILAN

German legend, was to be entered in a competition sponsored by the publishing house of Sozogno. *Le Villi* didn't win, but gained enough support among the musical intelligentsia to be reworked and produced at La Scala, Italy's leading Opera House, the following year. It was a success and Puccini was dubbed a young talent to watch. This success established Puccini with Italy's leading music publisher, Giulio Ricordi, who immediately commissioned a second opera from the young composer. With Fontana as librettist, Puccini set to work on *Edgar*. From the beginning, Puccini found the subject difficult and uninspiring. The bloody tale set in fourteenth century Flanders failed to evoke the composer's creative genius and he labored for five years to bring the work to the stage, much to the chagrin of his publisher, Ricordi, who was paying him a retainer.

Puccini was also beset with personal problems during this time. Not long after the premiere of *Le Villi,* his beloved mother died. The loss sent him reeling, coming as it did when her faith in his future was about to be vindicated and his subsequent depression affected his capacity to work. He became involved with Elvira Bonturi Gemignani, the wife of a prominent businessman in Lucca. She left her husband and young son for Puccini, bringing her elder daughter with her and in December of 1884, she bore Puccini his only child, Antonio. The people of Lucca were outraged and Puccini would never live there again. Years later, after the death of her husband, Elvira and Puccini finally married, but the passion of their affair had long since faded and their years together were characterized by bitterness. Having been a "ladies' man" since his youth, he responded to her total lack of support of his career and unwillingness to participate in his professional life by engaging in various extra marital relationships. He continued to pursue other women throughout his life, which only fueled the fires of Elvira's contempt.

Edgar premiered in 1889 and proved to be a dismal failure. While the press did acknowledge the same sparks of potential greatness Puccini had demonstrated in *Le Villi, Edgar* showed little of the anticipated growth in the definition of his style. Under pressure from his publishers to see a return on their investment, Puccini began searching for another subject. It was at this time, at Fontana's suggestion, that he first entertained Victorien Sardou's melodramatic *La Tosca* as an intriguing potential subject. Written as a vehicle

SARAH BERNHARDT
IN LA TOSCA, 1875

for the actress Sarah Bernhardt, it had premiered in Paris in 1887 and had proved to be incredibly successful. In the spring of 1889, it was enjoying a triumphant tour of Europe and Puccini eventually saw the play in 1890 and again in 1895. But, the French playwright either failed to see his play's operatic potential or was unwilling to grant the rights to an unknown young composer, so the idea was shelved.

Puccini turned instead to the Abbe Prevost novel, *L'Histoire de Manon Lescaut et du Chevalier des Grieux,* a subject already set for the operatic stage to great critical and public acclaim by the esteemed French composer, Jules Massanet. To venture a new setting of the same story was a huge risk, but the challenge seemed to fire Puccini's resolve. Determined not to repeat the failure of *Edgar,* Puccini now chose to trust his own dramatic instincts and he developed the habit of pursuing his librettists unmercifully until he had exactly the text he wanted. As a result, the libretto of Manon Lescaut consists of the work of seven different poets, including Ruggiero Leoncavallo, Marco Praga, Giuseppe Giacosa and Luigi Illica (the poets for Puccini's three best-known works, *La Boheme, Tosca* and *Madama Butterfly*), his publisher, Giulio Ricordi and even Puccini himself. When *Manon Lescaut* took the stage on February 1, 1893, there were a number of composers waiting to succeed Giuseppe Verdi as undisputed master of the Italian Operatic stage. Ricordi had placed his bet on Puccini, but Ruggiero Leoncavallo had gained notoriety with his *I Pagliacci;* Pietro Mascagni—a former college roommate of Puccini's—had achieved success with his *Cavalleria Rusticana* and Alfredo Catalani's *La Wally* had been highly acclaimed.

Manon Lescaut was a complete critical and popular triumph. The great potential hinted at in *Le Villi* and *Edgar* had finally been realized and the work took the stages of Europe by storm. Puccini was hailed by the press as Verdi's heir apparent and his years of financial uncertainty were over. Three years later to the day, on February 1, 1896, Puccini unveiled *La Boheme,* written with Illica and Giacosa. Based on Henri Murger's novella, *La Vie de Boheme,* the story follows the trials and triumphs of a group of starving young Parisian artists. The critics were not uniformly enthused, but the public almost immediately took the work to its heart. Within a year, the opera had been successfully produced on four continents. *La Boheme* became an indispensable part of the standard repertoire almost overnight—a standing it enjoys to this day. While still working on the score of La Boheme, Puccini again set his sights on Sardou's La Tosca. Since Sardou's initial refusal of the rights, however, Ricordi had secured the rights for an operatic setting by Alberto Franchetti, a composer who had achieved a modicum of success with his *Asrael* and *Cristoforo Colombo,* but whose contributions are all but forgotten today. Luigi Illica had already produced a libretto for Franchetti, which was greeted favorably by Sardou and even by Verdi, who had considered setting the play as an opera himself.

In a not altogether ethical series of maneuvers, Ricordi and Illica set about to convince Franchetti that *Tosca* was not well suited to his talents, thereby freeing the subject to be set by Puccini. They succeeded, the good-natured Franchetti released his rights to the subject and the winning team of Illica and Giacosa were set to work on a libretto of Tosca for Puccini. This was the third time the composer had chosen a subject already set by another musician or which had been claimed by another composer, which was the case with *La Boheme.* Ruggiero Leoncavallo had publicized his intent to set the Murger novel when Puccini announced his intent to write *La Boheme.* The result was an irreparable rift between the two artists who had worked together on the libretto for *Manon Lescaut*. Puccini's *La Boheme* was a great success while Leoncavallo's, produced some fifteen months later, suffered by comparison and has only received periodic revival since its premiere.

The rights secured, Puccini was slow to begin work on *Tosca*. Instead, he directed his energies toward travelling to oversee new productions of *La Boheme* in various European capitals, spending a particularly long period in Paris. He complained bitterly about his requisite social obligations and longed to return to the solitude of his Tuscan retreat, Torre del Lago. He was shy, felt socially inept in aristocratic circles and he learned during this period that his happiness relied on his deep connection with nature. His long stay in Paris, however, proved to be helpful, as he met and worked with Sardou on modifications to the play. Sardou was a lively character in his sixties whose stage works were extremely popular. He had a wonderful sense of what worked on the stage and he tended to write taut little melodramas with monochromatic characters and strong dramatic situations that hurdled them logically and inevitably toward often tragic ends. *Tosca* is no exception. A man is condemned to death due to his political affiliations; his lover implores the local authority to spare his life. The authority agrees to her request in exchange for her sexual favors for the night. She reluctantly agrees only to find that her lover is executed after all. Before the evening is over, all three major protagonists and a secondary character are dead. The famous Puccini biographer, Mosco Carner cites no fewer than five works from which Sardou could have plagiarized this essential plot line. After the play's premiere in 1887, two authors claimed that their work had been lifted. French playwright Ernest Daudet and American Maurice Barrymore had both written plays containing characters and situations strikingly similar to those found in Sardou's work.

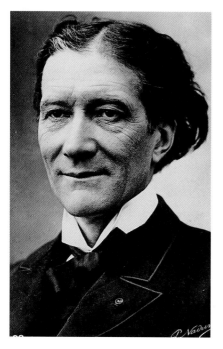

Sardou and Puccini got along famously. Both held each others' dramatic sense in high esteem and Puccini's suggestions for reducing the story from the original five to three acts were enthusiastically accepted. It was left to Luigi Illica to define the basic outline of the plot and the order of the dramatic action. This outline was then turned over to Giuseppe Giacosa to produce the verses, which the composer would set to music. Although the composer was still busy travelling and unprepared to begin work on *Tosca,* he regularly complained to Ricordi about the pace at which the libretto was being produced and the quality of the verses sent him by Giacosa. Giacosa disapproved of the subject, believing it was too violent and dramatic a plot for Puccini's lyrical gift and even offered to resign from the project. Puccini himself harbored some of the same reservations. A conversation recorded between Sardou and Puccini tells the story:

Puccini: Perhaps it would be better if a Frenchman were to set your play to music.

Sardou: No, better an Italian. *Tosca* is a Roman work. It needs your Italian song.

Puccini: Verdi, our great Verdi, once thought of *Tosca* and gave it up, a sign that the subject intimidated him. Do you wonder, M. Sardou, that I am afraid?

Sardou: Verdi wasn't intimidated, but Verdi is old, Verdi is tired....

Puccini: Alberto Franchetti also considered *Tosca* and gave it up in his turn.

Sardou: That, my dear maestro, certainly means nothing. Two men considered it; well, that is the best guarantee of *Tosca's* vitality.

Puccini: But my music is tenuous, it is delicate, it is written in a different register.

Sardou: There are no registers, M. Puccini, there's only talent!

Puccini: My previous heroines, Manon and Mimi, are different from Tosca.

Sardou: Manon, Mimi, Tosca, it is all the same thing!... Women in love all belong to the same family... They are all the same woman.

This comment tended to be true of both Sardou's and Puccini's heroines. The composer's fascination with women pervaded his personal and professional life. Seven of his twelve operas are named for their heroines. He perceived them to be fragile, like Mimi and Butterfly, or he perceived them to be strong and clever, like Tosca or Minnie in *The Girl of the Golden West*. But, he frequently perceived them to be victims of their fidelity to unscrupulous males. Eight of his major female characters die tragically for love.

Puccini finally set to work in earnest on the score in the spring of 1898, two years after the premiere of *La Boheme*. Puccini was deeply involved with revisions to the text, abandoning a second-act aria and quartet during Cavaradossi's torture at Scarpia's hand, which the composer felt was an obsolete operatic convention which detracted from the drama. The result is one of the most tension-filled scenes in opera. Puccini learned how to transcend pure lyricism and achieve real drama. Illica had also prepared an aria for Cavaradossi in Act III—a "farewell to life and love" of which the librettist was quite proud and which had been admired by Sardou and Verdi. Puccini found it too declamatory for a man facing the firing squad and replaced it with one of the opera's most famous arias, "E lucevan le stelle," which is short and powerful, expressing Cavaradossi's desperation at leaving the world and his love, Tosca. Puccini also changed the wording of several key lines to give them more color and punch. Even Sardou admitted the libretto was more powerful than his play.

Puccini also exercised his deepening interest in realistic atmospheric detail. He contacted musicians at the Vatican to find a text appropriate for the assembly to be muttering as they gathered behind Scarpia's monologue for the "Te Deum" at the close of Act I. Unable to find a liturgically appropriate prayer, he used a text he found in an old prayer book. He also requested the exact pitch of the largest bell at the Vatican, an "E" below the staff and traveled to Rome, climbed the parapet of the Castel Sant'Angelo and listened to the play of bells from the various Basilicas in Rome announcing Matins or morning prayer. He then recreated the sound in the opening of the Third Act. The composer contacted the Ministry of Education in Rome to secure authentic verses for the offstage shepherd boy's song in the third Act. This desire for realism was typical of the *verismo* style of his contemporaries. While Puccini's genius is considered to be more unique, *Tosca* is definitely one of his more "veristic" works in dramat-

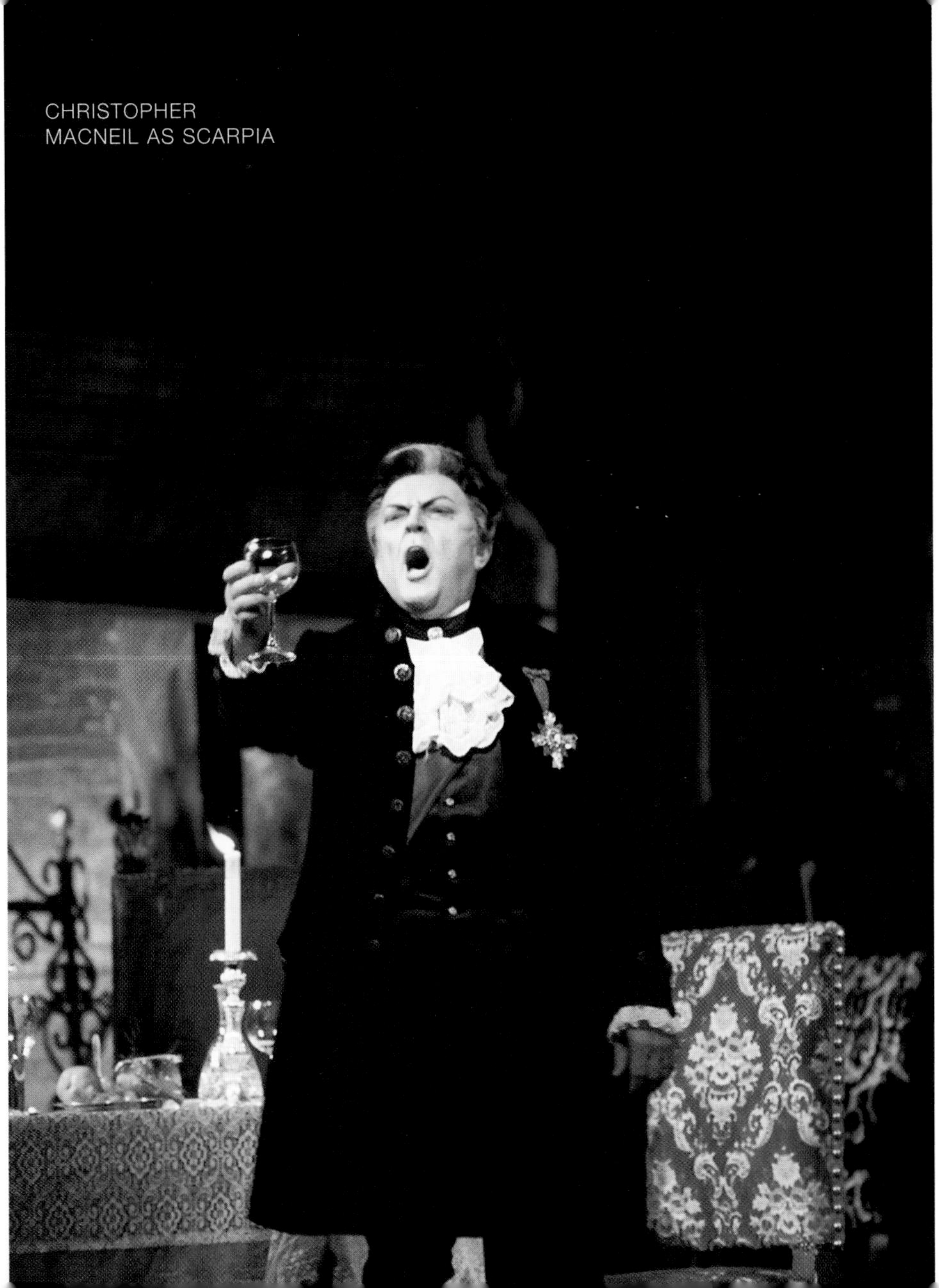

CHRISTOPHER
MACNEIL AS SCARPIA

ic content and musical treatment and his fascination with authentic atmosphere continued to enrich his operas in a variety of ways.

The score was finally delivered to Ricordi in October of 1899 and the publisher, always Puccini's greatest fan, found fault with the Tosca/Cavaradossi duet prior to the "fake" execution in the final Act. Ricordi found it fragmentary and objected to the use of music Puccini had written for the deleted Fourth Act of *Edgar*. Puccini, sure of his own dramatic sense, stood his ground and refused to make changes. At Illica's suggestion and since the action of the opera is set in Rome, Ricordi scheduled the premiere for January 14, 1900 at the Opera Costanzi in the Italian Capital. The production starred Hariclee Darclee as Tosca, Emilio DeMarchi as Cavaradossi and Eugenio Giraldoni as the villain, Scarpia. All of artists involved represented a new breed of singer/actor that eschewed the stilted acting style typical of most nineteenth-century Italian productions and sought a more dramatic physical portrayal in keeping with the *verismo* movement. The producer was Tito Ricordi, the publisher's son, who ran the preparatory proceedings with an iron hand and added intrigue to the premiere by banning the press and all interested observers from the rehearsals. Rumors began to spread that an anti-Puccini claque was planning to ruin the opening. There was a traditional antagonism between the cities of Northern and Southern Italy and Puccini had been derided in the Roman press as a 'flash in the pan'. To make matters worse, there was considerable political unrest at the time caused by difficult economic conditions. King Umberto I had dissolved the parliament the previous summer and there already had been two attempts on his life. The Queen and a number of government officials were to attend the premiere and there were rumors of a possible assassination attempt.

GAETAENE TEMMASINI, CONDUCTOR LEOPOLD MUGNONE AND GIOVANI CARUSO (BROTHER OF THE FAMOUS TENOR. ENRICO CARUSO)

Shortly before the curtain was to rise, the police approached Leopoldo Mugnone, the conductor and informed him of a bomb threat. If a bomb was to go off, he was to immediately have the orchestra play the national anthem. Needless to say, tensions ran high among the artists. Shortly after the opera began, there was uproar in the house. Mugnone, fearing for his life, fled the pit, but it was only an argument between some late arrivals and other patrons who had already taken their seats. The opera began again and ran without further disturbance.

The audience received the work warmly, but the press was not wholly convinced. They uniformly admired Puccini's treatment of the subject, but thought the libretto gruesome and unsuited to the operatic stage. They also admitted that the tension surrounding the opening precluded a truly objective evaluation of the work. As with many of Puccini's works, the press was soon silenced. *Tosca* was performed twenty more times that season at the Costanzi to sold-out houses and it was an overwhelming success with the public. Within a year, *Tosca* had conquered all the major houses of Italy, beginning with La Scala under Arturo Toscanini and moving quickly to all the capitals of Europe and beyond.

Tosca's three main protagonists have proven to be pivotal roles in the careers of a great many singers. Soprano Maria Jeritza was Puccini's favorite interpreter of the title role and was the first to deliver the famous second-act aria, "Vissi d'Arte" in a prone position after her scuffle with Scarpia. It has since become a convention to sing this aria from the floor. The great Toscas of this century have included Zinka Milanov, Renata Tebaldi and perhaps the most famous, Maria Callas, whose unerring sense of the stage made her Tosca legendary. All the great tenors of the twentieth century have portrayed Cavaradossi—from Caruso to Domingo and Scarpia is a standard for many great baritones—the most famous of which was probably Tito Gobbi, renowned for his stage presence, who triumphed repeatedly in the role in the 1950's and 1960's.

The musical intelligentsia of the time predicted Puccini's popularity would not last. They found his efforts too emotional, or too sensationalistic, lacking in depth, yet his works remain the backbone of the repertoire today for opera houses the world over because they speak directly to the human heart. As Baudelaire once said, "The autocrats in thought, the distributors of praise and blame, the monopolists of the things of the mind, have told you that you have no right to feel and enjoy—they are the Pharisees."

ENRICO CARUSO 1902

The Story of the Opera

ACT I

The opera begins in the church of Sant Andrea Della Valle. On the left is a platform before a covered painting in progress, surrounded by painter's tools; on the right is the gated private chapel of the Attavanti family.

We first hear the full orchestra thundering the motive representing Scarpia; the villainous chief of police and the curtain rises with unsettling descending chromatic figures in the orchestra. A figure furtively enters the stage. It is Angelotti, a fighter of the underground who has just escaped prison. His sister, the Marchesa Attavanti, has hidden a key for him to enter the family chapel to hide. He identifies his surroundings and after some difficulty, finds the key and enters the chapel gate.

The Sacristan enters. He is a comic figure with a nervous tic who speaks absent-mindedly of the painters' brushes he has been charged with keeping clean. He finally notices that the painter isn't there and remarks that he thought

LUCIANO PAVAROTTI AS CAVARADOSSI, 1985

he heard his footsteps. We hear the church bells ring the Angelus and the Sacristan dutifully kneels in prayer.

As his prayer comes to a close, the artist, Mario Cavaradossi enters and unveils his painting to continue his work. The sight of the painting startles the Sacristan who observes that it is of someone he knows. Cavaradossi says it is only the Virgin. Then the Sacristan remembers the face in the painting: it is the Marchesa Attavanti who has been coming daily to worship and Cavaradossi admits it is she. He explains that he has been observing her in secret and, finding her beautiful, has been reproducing her features in his rendering of the Virgin. In a shocked aside, the Sacristan comments on the sacrilege of presenting the Marchesa as a saint.

Mario begins to paint and in a famous aria, "Recondita armonia," he compares the face in his painting with his lover, Floria Tosca, a famous opera singer. He takes a small medallion from his pocket on which he keeps Tosca's image. He rhapsodizes about the blond haired, blue-eyed Marchesa compared with Tosca's dark beauty. He also sings about the beauty of her voice and concludes that the artist encounters many beauties, but his heart belongs to Tosca alone. All the while, the Sacristan mutters the prediction that the artist and his model will no doubt get together as the painting progresses and goes on to condemn such earthly goings on in a place of worship.

The Sacristan then draws Cavaradossi's attention to the lunch basket he has left for him and asks if he is going to eat. The artist replies he is not hungry and the Sacristan, with a greedy backward glance at the basket, tells Cavaradossi to be sure to lock up and takes his leave.

Angelotti, thinking the church is empty, approaches the gate and turns the key in the lock. Cavaradossi turns with a start. The escaped prisoner recognizes the artist, who also works secretly for the underground and expresses his gratitude for the promise of help, but Cavaradossi doesn't immediately recognize him. Angelotti steps from the shadows asking if prison has really changed him so radically. Suddenly, Cavaradossi identifies him as the governor of the overthrown republic and rushes to lock the side door. Cavaradossi no sooner offers his assistance to Angelotti than Tosca's voice is heard calling impatiently to Mario from outside the locked door. Angelotti retreats to the sanctuary of the chapel and Mario goes to admit her.

Tosca enters and looks around suspiciously. Spurning his attempted embrace, she asks why the door was locked, says she heard him speaking to someone and accuses him of being with the Marchesa. Mario calms her and declares his love, for which he receives a gentle reproach, as they are in a holy place. She then proceeds to lay a bouquet at the feet of a statue of the Madonna and kneel in prayer while Cavaradossi returns to his work.

Rising from her prayer, she asks if Mario could meet her that evening, explaining she has an early performance, but that they could then escape to his villa. Still preoccupied with Angelotti's presence in the nearby chapel, Mario responds absentmindedly and she is hurt. In a flirtatious aria, she describes the pleasures that await them at their secluded love nest and Mario is temporarily enslaved by her charm, but the romantic mood is suddenly broken as the chapel gate catches Cavaradossi's eye and he suddenly asks Tosca to leave him to his work. She responds with surprise, but turns to leave and sees the painting on which Mario is working.

Like the Sacristan, she is certain she has seen the lovely woman in the painting before and recognizes her as the beautiful Marchesa. In a fit of jealousy, she demands to know if Mario has been seeing her and if he is in love with her. He assures her that he has only seen her in prayer and has never even met her. She asks him to swear to it and he does, but Tosca is still haunted by her beautiful eyes. In soaring phrases, Cavaradossi assures Tosca that no eyes, no beauty could ever compare to hers. Her jealousy is somewhat assuaged, but still she asks him to paint her blue eyes dark. Mario lovingly teases her about her jealousy and she acquiesces but says that he must forgive her, seeing how she is tormented. Their voices join in a radiant expression of their love for one another.

PLACIDO DOMINGO
(CAVARADOSSI) AND
HELEN BEHRENS
(TOSCA) 1985

Gently, Mario again insists she must leave so he can work. She asks him to promise that no woman will come to speak to him as he works, not even praying. He promises, but just before she leaves, she admonishes him once more to paint the lady's eyes dark. With Tosca gone, Cavaradossi rushes to the chapel to release Angelotti, who explains that he is planning to either leave the country or stay in hiding in Rome and that his sister was to have left a complete ladies wardrobe for him hidden under the altar. Together they find the disguise: a cloak, a bonnet and a fan. Mario comments that the ardor he saw in the Marchesa's eyes as she prayed was clearly love for her brother. Angelotti responds that she would stop at nothing to save him from Scarpia and his agents. Cavaradossi reviles Scarpia, who uses his position as a government official for his own lecherous gains and vows that Angelotti will be saved.

The artist encourages his friend not to wait until dark to escape and explains how he can reach his villa undetected. Should there be trouble there, he can hide in a niche halfway down the shaft of the well on the property.

Suddenly, there is a cannon blast announcing the escape of a prisoner. Hands clasped in a final vow to defeat the oppressors, the two dissidents make their escape.

The Sacristan enters excitedly and is surprised to find Cavaradossi has gone. He is soon followed by hordes of choirboys, acolytes and monks entering from all sides. He tells them that Bonaparte has been defeated in a battle and that the victory will be celebrated with a solemn *Te Deum* and a new cantata to be sung by Floria Tosca. They all burst into loud song and dance at the news, but the festive tone is cut short by the sudden arrival of Scarpia, followed by his henchman, Spoletta and several police.

He angrily orders them to go and vest for the *Te Deum* and all slink away silently. Scarpia detains the Sacristan, informing him of Angelotti's escape and that the fugitive has been traced to the church. He brusquely orders the police to search the premises and asks the Sacristan the location of the Attavanti Chapel. He points it out and expresses alarm that the gate is ajar. They enter briefly and emerge with Scarpia holding the fan meant to be part of Angelotti's disguise. Examining it, Scarpia identifies the crest of the Marchesa Attavanti and turning sees Cavaradossi's painting of the Marchesa in the guise of the Virgin. The Sacristan identifies Cavaradossi as the artist and Scarpia muses that he knows Cavaradossi to be a member of the resistance and Tosca's lover

The Sacristan then notices the basket which he finds empty and, under interrogation, confesses that he doesn't know how it got in the chapel and that Cavaradossi had said he wasn't hungry. Scarpia quickly concludes that Angelotti ate the lunch and escaped—with help from the painter.

Tosca enters, distractedly looking for Mario. On seeing her, Scarpia hides and muses that the fan he holds may serve the same purpose as Iago's handkerchief in sparking her jealousy. The Sacristan tells her Mario is gone and exits nervously. Her suspicions of his infidelity are aroused.

Scarpia oozes out from the shadows and approaches Tosca, offering her holy water to bless herself. He praises her for her art and her devotion, saying that when she comes to church, she comes to pray, unlike others who come for a lovers' rendezvous. Tosca asks what he is implying and he produces the fan with the Attavanti crest, asking if it is typical of a painters tools. Tosca is reduced to tears of jealous rage and swears revenge on her rival. Scarpia responds with alarm at such outburst in a holy place. She answers that she will be forgiven when the Lord sees her pain and Scarpia escorts her to the door.

Spoletta emerges from the shadows and Scarpia orders him to follow Tosca, sure that she will lead them to Cavaradossi and Angelotti. He is to report back to Scarpia at the Palazzo Farnese. In the background, the crowd is gathering for the Te Deum. Against the background of the religious celebration, Scarpia sings of his lust for Tosca and that the jealous passion he has aroused in her will turn into a passionate embrace. He shall have both the lovers—Cavaradossi hanging from the gallows and Tosca in his arms.

ACT II

Scarpia is dining alone in his apartment in the Palazzo Farnese. Music can be heard from the courtyard below his open window—it is the celebration in honor of General Melas' reported victory over Napoleon. Scarpia rings for his assistant, Sciarrone. Upon entering, he is ordered to tell Tosca that Scarpia wishes to see her after the cantata she is soon to perform. Scarpia sends a note to be delivered to the diva. Alone again, Scarpia voices his creed regarding love. He cares nothing for love's tenderness, preferring to take what he desires by force, then discard it.

Spoletta enters and nervously reports that they followed Tosca to Cavaradossi's villa, but did not find Angelotti. Scarpia berates him violently, but his fury subsides when Spoletta relates that they arrested Cavaradossi. Scarpia then calls for the painter to be brought before him, along with the executioner Roberti, a judge and a clerk. Tosca's voice is heard rising in the cantata from the courtyard as Mario is brought in. He demands to know why he has been arrested. He is questioned about Angelotti, but denies any knowledge of the escapee's whereabouts. The cantata accompanies the interrogation, but is abruptly cut off when Scarpia, out of patience, slams the window shut. Scarpia continues to question the painter with increasing violence, but Mario will not respond.

Suddenly, Tosca bursts into the room and embraces Mario. Scarpia orders that the dissident be taken to the adjoining room where the judge will take his confession. He leaves accompanied by Roberti, the judge and the clerk and Sciarrone. Spoletta remains guarding the door.

Resuming a casual tone, Scarpia questions Tosca about the villa and she responds that only Mario was there. He then calls to Sciaronne, asking if the painter has confessed. Sciaronne replies that he has not. Tosca, unaware that her lover has been taken to a torture chamber, tells Scarpia that Mario will never confess. Scarpia calmly tells her that her honesty would save her lover pain, that even now his head is surrounded by a spiked steel band that is being tightened with every denial. Mario is heard groaning from behind the door.

Tosca calls to Mario through the door, but he responds that she is to remain silent. She angrily turns on Scarpia, condemning his brutality, but Scarpia responds by ordering Spoletta to open the door. Tosca is horrified at the sight of the torture. Scarpia angrily demands the whereabouts of Angelotti. Tosca pleads with Mario to allow her to speak, but he refuses amid cries of pain. Unable to bear the sight of her lover's torment, she blurts out that Angelotti is hidden in the well at the villa. Scarpia orders the torture stopped and the artist, unconscious and bloody, is brought back into the room and placed on a couch. Tosca, sobbing, rushes to his side. As he regains consciousness, Mario asks if she has revealed the secret and she responds that she hasn't. At that moment Scarpia announces Angelotti's location to his henchmen.

Furiously, Mario curses Tosca for betraying his trust and at that moment, Sciarrone enters to report that Napoleon has defeated General Melas at Marengo. In an ecstatic delirium, Mario exults over the victory, ignoring Tosca's efforts to quiet him. Scarpia declares his loathing for the artist and orders him sent away to the gallows. Clinging desperately to Mario, Tosca attempts to keep them from taking him away but is separated from him and ordered to stay.

Tosca sits desolate by the door as Scarpia smugly returns to his unfinished meal. He offers her a glass of wine and suggests that together they may yet find a way to save her Mario. Her voice filled with contempt, she asks him the price for her lover's life. He responds that, though he has the reputation of a mercenary, when a beautiful woman is involved, he doesn't stoop to talk of money—price is Tosca herself.

She recoils in horror, but to the sound of distant drumming, he describes the impending execution to her. Her lover will not see the sunrise tomorrow and because of her refusal he will die. Overcome with grief, Tosca sings her famous aria, "Vissi d'Arte," recalling her life of art and faith and generous care for the poor, asking God why he would repay her in this way.

She pleads for mercy and Scarpia responds that for one night of love, she may have her Mario restored to her. Spoletta enters to report that Angelotti was found, but he poisoned himself upon his arrest. Scarpia orders the corpse hung from the gallows and then inquires about Cavaradossi, to which Spoletta responds they will proceed as ordered, but Scarpia detains him and, turning to Tosca, asks her intentions. She nods her assent, but asks for a guarantee of Mario's release.

Scarpia says he has never granted a pardon—that they must make it seem as though the artist has been put to death and that Spoletta would see to the details. In her presence he orders Spoletta to stage the execution "Just as we did with Palmieri." Knowingly, Spoletta repeats the phrase as he leaves the room.

Tosca is given permission to go to Mario and inform him of the mock execution. She also extracts the promise of safe passage for them both to leave the city and while Scarpia is at his desk writing out the passport, Tosca moves to the table to get her glass of wine and surreptitiously picks up a knife. Hiding it behind her, she turns to see Scarpia approach her with outstretched arms. As he embraces her, she plunges the knife in his chest. The villain dies at her feet as he pleads for mercy. Staring at Scarpia's lifeless body, she washes her fingers with some water and a napkin, then looking around for the passport, she sees it clenched in Scarpia's fist. She removes it from his hand and places it in her bodice. With the disdainful comment, "Before him, all Rome trembled," she turns to leave, but changes her mind. She lights two candles, placing them on either side of Scarpia's head and removes a crucifix from the wall and places it on his chest. Then quietly, Tosca steals into the night.

ACT III

The scene is the rampart of the Castel Sant'Angelo. To the side, a cell. It is night and in the distance we hear a shepherd's song. Dawn begins to break slowly as Matins is rung from the churches of Rome. Cavaradossi is led to his cell where his name is registered. The jailer informs him that he has an hour to live and asks if he wishes to see a priest. Mario refuses, but offers the jailer a ring in exchange for the promise to deliver a farewell letter to his love. The jailer agrees and departs.

Mario sits to write his farewell to Tosca, but overcome by memories, he interrupts his writing and pours out his grief in the plaintive aria, "E lucevan le stelle," recalling the beauty of their nights of love. They are joys he will never know again and now he is to die in desperation.

Tosca is admitted to his cell. She excitedly shows him Scarpia's order for their safe passage out of the country, but seeing Scarpia's signature, he is taken aback. She recounts the drama of Scarpia's proposal, her denial, her ultimate agreement and his murder at her hand. In awe of her courage, Mario caresses her hands—hands so gentle and pure, yet hands that killed for love of him.

She anxiously explains about the mock execution—that they will fire blank rounds, but that he is to fall convincingly in death, when they fire, to avoid any suspicion. They join their voices in a rapturous vision of their impending freedom together, reaffirming their undying love.

The officer approaches to tell Mario it is time for the execution. In hushed tones, Tosca reminds him to fall convincingly and not to get up until she tells him; "...like Tosca in the theatre," he says with a smile.

Having said their farewell, Mario follows the guards as Tosca remains in the cell watching them move to the platform. Mario is led to the far wall. He refuses a blindfold offered him and the guards move into firing position. Tosca comments nervously about how long it is taking. At last they are ready. The guards fire and Mario falls to the ground. Tosca comments on how effectively Mario has handled this acting assignment. Slowly the officials inspect and cover the body and leave the area.

When all have gone, Tosca calls to Mario, softly at first, then more insistently as he fails to respond, she approaches and finds that he is really dead. She reels back in horror as the sound of an angry mob is heard from downstairs. Scarpia's body has been found and the police are coming to seize Tosca for his murder. She runs to the top of the parapet, with Spoletta and the others in hot pursuit. He grabs her, screaming that she will pay for Scarpia's life. She wildly pushes him away and, standing atop the parapet, she cries, "Scarpia, we meet before God!" With that, she flings herself over the edge and falls to her death.

The Performers

&

Renata Scotto (Floria Tosca) Scotto, a native of Savona, Italy, began her vocal studies as a mezzo-soprano. She moved to Milan at age 16 and under the guidance of Mercedes Llopart became a soprano. A competition win afforded her the opportunity to debut in her home town in 1952, as Violetta in Verdi's *La Traviata.* The following year, she repeated the role at the Teatro Nuovo in Milan, followed a year later by her La Scala debut in the secondary role of Walter in Catalani's *La Wally.* Abandoning the famous house for the opportunity to perform leading roles in smaller houses, she continued to develop her craft until she was seen on the stages of Rome, Venice and finally in London—where she debuted as Mimi in Puccini's *La Boheme* in 1957. In that same year, her career finally received the ultimate boost when she performed the difficult role of Amina in Bellini's *La Sonnambula* on three days' notice, substituting for an indisposed Maria Callas. She returned to *La Scala* as a star, and before long was heard in all the major houses on both sides of the

Atlantic, as well as in Japan—where she was the first to portray the title role in Donizetti's Lucia di Lammermoor.

Early in her career, her repertoire was dominated by bel canto roles including Lucia, Amina, Adina in Donizetti's L'Elisir d'Amore, and the title role in Bellini's *Norma*. American audiences came to know her best in her portrayals of Puccini and Verdi heroines. She made her American debut in 1960 at the Chicago Lyric Opera as Mimi, and in 1965 at New York's Metropolitan Opera as Cio-Cio-San in Puccini's *Madama Butterfly*. In the following years, she continued to expand her repertoire to include more *spinto* roles including the heavier Verdi roles and classics from the *verismo* repertoire like Maddalena in Giordano's *Andrea Chenier* and the title role in Cilea's *Adriana Lecouvreur*. She was the first to sing all three heroines in Puccini's *Il Trittico,* (three one-act operas) in one evening at the MET and the first to sing both Mimi and Musetta in *La Boheme* in the same season at the MET.

Puccini continued to figure prominently in her career as she made her directing debut with *Madama Butterfly* at the MET in 1987. Recently, her repertoire has expanded to include a number of German works, the Marschalin in Strauss' *Der Rosenkavalier* and several Wagnerian roles among them. She now divides her time between singing, directing, and teaching in master classes in Europe and America.

Scotto is known not only for the beauty and versatility of her voice, but for her outstanding dramatic portrayals. Her recorded repertoire boasts over 25 complete operas, and

Puccini's heroines figure prominently in her catalogue. She is one of the great singing actresses of our age and she portrays the diva, Tosca, with unparalleled strength, tenderness and understanding.

Placido Domingo (Mario Cavaradossi) Placido Domingo is one of the brightest stars the opera has produced in the twentieth century. Born in Madrid in 1941, his family moved to Mexico in 1950. His early musical studies included piano, conducting and finally singing. He began his career as a baritone, singing *zarzuela,* a semi-operatic Mexican form of musical theatre in which his family was deeply involved. His first major operatic role was Alfredo in *Verdi's La Traviata,* sung in Monterrey, Mexico in 1961. That same year he made is American debut in Dallas as Arturo in Donizetti's *Lucia di Lammermoor.*

He spent the next four years singing with the Israel National Opera where he sang some 300 performances of ten different roles, most of them in Hebrew. In 1965 he made his debut at the New York City Opera as Pinkerton in *Puccini's Madama Butterfly,* and demonstrated his versatility the following year in the title role of the first North American performance of Ginastera's Don Rodrigo. 1968 saw his triumphant Metropolitan Opera Debut as Maurizio in Cilea's *Adriana Lecouvreur.* He has been a favorite of American audiences ever since.

He has sung in all the major opera houses of the world, and his repertoire includes over 100 roles, ranging from Mozart's *Idomeneo* to the title role in Menotti's Goya, a role he created in Washington DC in 1986. He has recorded extensively, showing a particular fondness for the great Verdi and Puccini roles, and is considered the finest living interpreter of Verdi's Otello. In recent years he has included Wagner's Lohengrin, Parsifal, and Siegmund to his highly eclectic repertoire with great success, and is equally at home in French opera, including Saint-Saens' Samson and Bizet's Don Jose in *Carmen* to his triumphs.

Not content to only sing opera, he has maintained a thriving career as an opera conductor since the 1980's, and has also served as artistic director for the Los Angeles Music Center Opera and the Washington Opera, enhancing the lot of both companies with his vast experience, dedication and generous involvement. He has also done a great deal to increase opera's popularity, having recorded many non-operatic albums including duets with the late John Denver

PLACIDO DOMINGO, 1997

and several albums of popular and zarzuela songs. He is also well-known for his participation in the "3 Tenors" concerts and recordings in which he collaborated with colleague Luciano Pavarotti and fellow Spaniard, Jose Carreras.

He continues to be a force in promoting up-and-coming artists by sponsoring Operalia, a worldwide singing competition established in 1993. Through his deep involvement and wide influence in the world of opera, he has managed to launch the careers of a number of artists.

Highly energetic and versatile, he is widely regarded as the greatest lyric-dramatic tenor of our time. The role of Cavaradossi was the vehicle for his Covent Garden debut in 1971, and he has recorded it twice and performed it countless times on stage. The warmth, intelligence and passion of his portrayal is unequaled, and his commitment to the character is evident in every phrase of this exceptional performance.

Renato Bruson (Baron Scarpia) Bruson was born in the small Italian village of Este, not far from Padua. He studied voice in Padua and made his debut in Spoleto in 1961 as the Conte di Luna in Verdi's *Il Trovatore.* He spent the next severalyears appearing with great success in the many smaller houses n Italy, then went on to debut at the Metropolitan Opera in New York in 1969, singing the role of Enrico Ashton in Donizetti's *Lucia di Lammermoor.*

He continued to appear in New York for many years—specializing in the great Verdi baritone roles—and went on to conquer the stages of the world's major houses including Vienna, Berlin, Munich, Chicago, San Francisco and Los Angeles, where he first performed the title role in Verdi's brilliant comedy, *Falstaff.*

Besides the Verdi roles, many of which he has recorded, he has also contributed much to a thorough exploration of Donizetti's works, having sung in revivals of his *Belisario, Gemma di Vergy, Les Martyrs, Le Duc d'Albe, Torquato Tasso, Caterina Cornaro* and *La Favorita*. He has also been acclaimed for his portrayals of Scarpia, the role heard here and the title role in Mozart's *Don Giovanni*.

Known for the beauty of his phrasing and the strength and focus of his sizeable voice, he has always proven himself a formidable stage presence—especially in portraying the more noble characters such as Verdi's *Simon Boccanegra*. Scarpia is a figure of similar weight and Bruson's insightful performance heard on this disc is powerful and definitive.

James Levine (conductor) Maestro Levine is one of the most influential figures in American opera in this century. Born in Cincinnati, Ohio in 1943, he was a virtual prodigy at the piano, making his solo concerto debut with the Cincinnati Symphony Orchestra at the age of ten. Later, while studying at the Julliard School in New York, he gradually turned his attention to conducting, studying under Jean Morel, Alfred Wallenstein and the esteemed Fausto Cleva.

From 1964-70 he served as assistant conductor of the Cleveland Orchestra under the famous George Szell, where he also built a successful student orchestra program at the Cleveland Institute.

His opera conducting debut took place in 1970 with the San Francisco Opera with *Tosca,* the work heard here, and debuted in 1971 with the Metropolitan Opera, again conducting *Tosca*. His success in this debut led to his appointment in 1973 as principal conductor at the MET, and eventually in 1976 as Music Director at America's most famous opera house. Since then, he has conducted over 1500 performances of a wide variety of repertoire at the

MET.

In 1986, he became Artistic Director, and his tenure has proven to be one of the most successful in the MET's long and distinguished history. While maintaining the integrity of the standard Verdi, Puccini and Wagner repertoire at the historic house, he has also successfully ventured into less familiar territory, including Gershwin's *Porgy and Bess,* Kurt Weill's *The Rise and Fall of the City of Mahagonny,* and Alban Berg's *Lulu* to the MET's repertoire. He has also successfully commissioned new works for the revered house, including the John Corigliano's innovative The Ghosts of Versailles.

He has recorded extensively, beginning with Verdi's obscure *Giovanna d'Arco* in 1972, and including a highly acclaimed recording of Wagner's *Ring Cycle* in the late 1980's. Under his baton, the Metropolitan Opera Orchestra has become regarded as the finest opera orchestra in the world, and he has conducted in many of the world's most renowned venues, including Bayreuth, home of Wagner's legacy.

In recent years, he has expanded on his operatic success by returning frequently to the piano as a collaborative artist in concerts and recordings with the worlds great singers and instrumentalists.

His unparalleled intelligence and high energy have always produced intense and intriguing readings of both the new and the old in the operatic repertoire, and this reading of *Tosca,* the work that began his meteoric rise to operatic immortality, is no exception.

The Libretto

Act 1

THE CHURCH OF SANT'ANDREA DELLA VALLE

(To the right, the Attavanti chapel. To the left, a painter's scaffold with a large painting covered with cloth. Painter's tools. A basket. Enter Angelotti in prisoner's clothes, dishevelled, tired, and shaking with fear, nearly running. He looks quickly about.)

CD 1/Track 1   The full orchestra blares its three-measure introduction — it is Scarpia's theme. **(00:15)** The curtain rises to an energetic theme signifying Angelotti's flight from the authorities.

ANGELOTTI
Ah! Finalmente! Nel terror mio stolto
vedea ceffi di birro in ogni volto.

ANGELOTTI
Ah! At last! In my stupid fear I thought
I saw a policeman's jowl in every face.

stops to look around more attentively, calmer now that he recognises the place. Sighs with relief as he notices the column with its basin of Holy Water and the Madonna.

La pila...la colonna...
"A piè della Madonna"
mi scrisse mia sorella...

The column...and the basin...
"At the base of the Madonna"
my sister wrote me...

goes up to the Madonna and searches about at the base. He gives a muffled shout of joy as he picks up the key.

Ecco la chiave, ed ecco la cappella!

This is the key, and this is the chapel!

With the utmost care, he puts the key in the lock of the Attavanti chapel, opens the gate, goes in, closes the gate and disappears within. Enter the sacristan from the rear, carrying a bunch of painter's brushes, and muttering loudly as though he were addressing someone.

(02:13) We first hear the Sacristan's theme which immediately identifies him as a "buffo" or comic character.

SAGRESTANO
E sempre lava! Ogni pennello è sozzo
peggio d'un collarin d'uno scagnozzo.
Signor pittore...Tò!

SACRISTAN
Forever washing! And every brush is filthier
than an urchin's collar.
Mister Painter...There!

looks toward the scaffold with its painting and is surprised on seeing nobody there

Nessuno. Avrei giurato
che fosse ritornato
il cavalier Cavaradossi.

No one...I would have sworn
the Cavalier Cavaradossi
had come back.

puts down the brushes, mounts the scaffold and examines the basket, remarking:

No, sbaglio,
il paniere è intatto.

No, I'm mistaken.
The basket has not been touched.

The Angelus sounds. The sacristan kneels and prays in hushed voice.

Angelus Domini nuntiavit Mariae,
et concepit de Spiritu Sancto.
Ecce ancilla Domini;
fiat mihi secundum Verbum tuum
et Verbum caro factum est
et habitavit in nobis...

Angelus Domini nuntiavit Mariae,
Et concepit de Spiritu Sancto.
Ecce ancilla Domini;
Fiat mihi secundum Verbum tuum
Et Verbum caro factum est
Et habitavit in nobis...

Enter Cavaradossi from the side door and sees the sacristan kneeling.

CAVARADOSSI
Che fai?

CAVARADOSSI
What are you doing?

SAGRESTANO (*alzandosi*)
Recito L'Angelus.

SACRISTAN (*rising*)
Reciting the Angelus.

Cavaradossi mounts the scaffold and uncovers the painting: it is of a Mary Magdalene with great blue eyes and a cascade of golden hair. The painter stands in silence before it and studies it closely. The sacristan turns to speak to Cavaradossi and cries out in amazement as he sees the uncovered picture.

Sante ampolle!
Il suo ritratto!

Oh holy vessels!
Her picture!

CAVARADOSSI
Di chi?

CAVARADOSSI
Whose?

SAGRESTANO
Di quell'ignota
che i dì passati a pregar qui venìa.
Tutta devota...e pia.

SACRISTAN
That strange girl who has been coming here
these past few days to pray.
Such devotion...such piety.

waves towards the Madonna from whose base Angelotti has taken the key

CAVARADOSSI
È vero. E tanto ell'era
infervorata nella sua preghiera
ch'io ne pinsi, non visto, il bel sembiante.

CAVARADOSSI
It is so. And she was so absorbed
in fervent prayer that I could paint
her lovely face unnoticed.

SAGRESTANO (*fra sé*)
Fuori, Satana, fuori!

SACRISTAN (*to himself*)
Away, Satan, away!

CAVARADOSSI
Dammi i colori.

CAVARADOSSI
Give me my paints.

The sacristan does so. Cavaradossi paints rapidly, with frequent pauses to observe his work. The sacristan comes and goes; he carries a small basin in which he continues his job of washing the brushes. Suddenly Cavaradossi leaves his painting: from his pocket he takes a medallion with a portrait in miniature, and his eyes travel from the miniature to his own work.

Recondita armonia
di bellezze diverse! È bruna Floria,
l'ardente amante mia...

SAGRESTANO *(fra sé)*
Scherza coi fanti e lascia stare i santi...

Oh hidden harmony
of contrasting beauties! Floria
is dark. my love and passion...

SACRISTAN *(to himself)*
Jest with knaves and neglect the saints...

CD 1/Track 2   In this famous aria, "Recondita armonia" Cavaradossi reflects on the beauty of Tosca compared with the beauty of the woman in his painting. This aria is a favorite of tenors and is frequently performed in concert.

CAVARADOSSI
E te, beltade ignota...
cinta di chiome bionde,
tu azzurro hai l'occhio,
Tosca ha l'occhio nero!

SAGRESTANO *(fra sé)*
Scherza coi fanti e lascia stare i santi...

CAVARADOSSI
L'arte nel suo mistero
le diverse bellezze insiem confonde;
ma nel ritrar costei
il mio solo pensiero, Tosca, sei tu!

SAGRESTANO *(fra sé, in disparte)*
Queste diverse gonne
che fanno concorrenza alle Madonne
mandan tanfo d'inferno.
Scherza coi fanti e lascia stare i santi.
Ma con quei cani di volterriani,
nemici del santissimo governo,
non c'è da metter voce!
Scherza coi fanti e lascia stare i santi,
già, sono impenitenti tutti quanti!

CAVARADOSSI
And you, mysterious beauty...
Crowned with blond locks.
Your eyes are blue
and Tosca's black!

SACRISTAN *(to himself)*
Jest with knaves and neglect the saints...

CAVARADOSSI
Dissimilar beauties are together blended
by the mystery of art:
yet as I paint her portrait, Tosca,
my sole thought is of you.

SACRISTAN *(to himself)*
These various women
in rivalry with the Madonna
smell of the devil.
Jest with knaves and neglect the saints...
But we can have no truck
with these agnostic dogs.
Enemies of the Holy Government!
Jest with knaves and neglect the saints...
Yes, they are sinners the whole pack of them!

Facciam piuttosto il segno della croce.
(a Cavaradossi)
Eccellenza, vado?

CAVARADOSSI
Fa il tuo piacere!
(Continua a dipingere.)

SAGRESTANO
Pieno è il paniere...
Fa penitenza?

CAVARADOSSI
Fame non ho.

SAGRESTANO *(con ironia, stropicciandosi le mani)*
Oh! Mi rincresce!

Let us rather make the sign of the cross.
(to Cavaradossi)
Excellency, may I go?

CAVARADOSSI
As you wish.
(resumes his painting)

SACRISTAN
Your basket's full...
Are you fasting?

CAVARADOSSI
I'm not hungry.

SACRISTAN *(ironically rubbing his hands)*
Oh! So sorry!

He cannot contain a gleeful gesture as he glances avidly at the full basket. He picks it up and places it to one side.

Badi, quand'esce chiuda.

CAVARADOSSI
Va!

SAGRESTANO
Vo.

Be sure to close up when you leave.

CAVARADOSSI
Run along!

SACRISTAN
I'm going.

Exit at the rear. Cavaradossi continues working, his back to the chapel. Angelotti appears at the gate there, and puts the key in the lock, believing the church is still deserted.

CAVARADOSSI
(al cigolio della serratura si volta)
Gente là dentro!

CAVARADOSSI
(turns at the creaking of the lock)
Someone in there!

Startled by the painter's movement, Angelotti stops as though to return to his hiding-place, but looks up and cries out in joy as he recognises Cavaradossi. Smothering his cry, he stretches out his arms towards the painter as toward an unexpected friend in need.

ANGELOTTI
Voi! Cavaradossi!
Vi manda Iddio!
Non mi ravvisate?
Il carcere mi ha dunque assai mutato.

ANGELOTTI
You! Cavaradossi!
Heaven itself has sent you!
Don't you recognise me?
Has prison, then, wrought such a great
change in me?

CAVARADOSSI

CAVARADOSSI

looks closely at Angelotti's face and finally remembers. Quickly drops his palette and brushes, and comes down from the scaffold. He looks about warily as he goes up to Angelotti.

Angelotti! Il Console
della spenta repubblica romana!
(Corre a chiudere la porta a destra.)

Angelotti! The Consul!
Of the lamented Roman Republic!
(runs to close door at right)

ANGELOTTI
Fuggii pur ora da Castel Sant'Angelo.

ANGELOTTI
I have just escaped from Castel Sant'Angelo.

CAVARADOSSI
Disponete di me.

CAVARADOSSI
I am at your service.

TOSCA *(fuori)*
Mario!

TOSCA *(from without)*
Mario!

At Tosca's call, Cavaradossi motions Angelotti to be quiet.

CAVARADOSSI
Celatevi! È una donna gelosa.
Un breve istante e la rimando.

CAVARADOSSI
Go and hide! It's a jealous woman!
Only a moment and I'll send her away.

TOSCA
Mario!

CAVARADOSSI
(verso la porta da dove viene la voce)
Eccomi!

ANGELOTTI
(colto da un accesso di debolezza, si appoggia all'impalcato)
Sono stremo di forze; più non reggo.

CAVARADOSSI

fetches the basket from the top of the scaffold and pushes Angelotti towards the chapel with words of encouragement

In questo panier v'è cibo e vino.

ANGELOTTI
Grazie!

CAVARADOSSI
Presto!

Angelotti enters the chapel.

TOSCA
Mario!

CAVARADOSSI
(in the direction of her voice)
Here I am.

ANGELOTTI
(feeling suddenly weak, he leans against the scaffold)
I'm faint with exhaustion. I can't stand up.

CAVARADOSSI

There's food and wine in this basket.

ANGELOTTI
Thanks!

CAVARADOSSI
Quick now!

CD 1/Track 4 As Tosca is admitted, she goes to place flowers before a statue of the virgin and we hear the theme associated with her piety. It will become the theme of her most celebrated aria, "Vissi d'arte" in the second act. As she tries to lure Mario from his work, she describes their weekend getaway in a charming aria, "Non la sospiri." **(02:58)**

TOSCA *(sempre fuori, chiamando stizzita)*
Mario! Mario! Mario!

TOSCA *(still from without, calling angrily)*
Mario! Mario! Mario!

CAVARADOSSI *(apre il cancello)*
Son qui.

TOSCA

bursts in with a kind of violence, thrusting Cavaradossi aside as he tries to embrace her, and looks around suspiciously

Perché chiuso?

CAVARADOSSI
Lo vuole il sagrestano.

TOSCA
A chi parlavi?

CAVARADOSSI
A te!

TOSCA
Altre parole bisbigliavi.
Ov'è?...

CAVARADOSSI
Chi?

TOSCA
Colei!...Quella donna!
Ho udito i lesti
passi e un fruscio di vesti...

CAVARADOSSI
Sogni!

TOSCA
Lo neghi?

CAVARADOSSI *(opening the gate)*
I am here...

TOSCA

Why was it locked?

CAVARADOSSI
That was the sacristan's wish.

TOSCA
With whom were you talking?

CAVARADOSSI
With you!

TOSCA
You were whispering with someone else.
Where is she?...

CAVARADOSSI
Who?

TOSCA
She! That woman!
I heard her quick steps
and her dress rustling.

CAVARADOSSI
You're dreaming!

TOSCA
Do you deny it?

CAVARADOSSI *(fa per baciarla)*
Lo nego e t'amo!

TOSCA *(con dolce rimprovero)*
Oh! Innanzi alla Madonna.
No, Mario mio!
Lascia pria che la preghi che l'infiori.

She approaches the Madonna, arranges artfully about her the flowers she has brought, and kneels to pray; then rises to address Mario who has resumed his work.

Ora stammi a sentir; stasera canto,
ma è spettacolo breve. Tu m'aspetti
sull'uscio della scena
e alla tua villa andiam soli, soletti.

CAVARADOSSI *(che fu sempre soprappensiero)*
Stasera?

TOSCA
È luna piena
e il notturno effluvio floreal
inebria il cor. Non sei contento?

CAVARADOSSI *(ancora un po' distratto e pensieroso)*
Tanto!

TOSCA *(colpita da quell'accento)*
Tornalo a dir!

CAVARADOSSI
Tanto!

TOSCA
Lo dici male.

CAVARADOSSI *(trying to kiss her)*
I deny it and I love you!

TOSCA *(with gentle reproach)*
Oh no! Before the gentle Madonna,
no, Mario!
First let me pray and offer these flowers.

Now listen: tonight I am singing,
but the programme will be brief. Wait for me
at the stage entrance, and we two shall go
alone together to your villa.

CAVARADOSSI *(his thoughts still elsewhere)*
Tonight?

TOSCA
It is the time of the full moon,
when the heart is drunk with the nightly
fragrance of the flowers. Are you not happy?

CAVARADOSSI *(still somewhat distraught and thoughtful)*
So very happy!

TOSCA *(struck by his tone)*
Say it again!

CAVARADOSSI
So very happy!

TOSCA
How faintly you say it!

sits on the steps next to Cavaradossi

Non la sospiri, la nostra casetta
che tutta ascosa nel verde ci aspetta?
Nido a noi sacro, ignoto al mondo
inter,
pien d'amore e di mister?
Al tuo fianco sentire
per le silenziose
stellate ombre, salir
le voci delle cose!
Dai boschi, dai roveti,
dall'arse erbe, dall'imo
dei franti sepolcreti
odorosi di timo.
La notte escon bisbigli
di minuscoli amori
e perfidi consigli
che ammolliscono i cuori.
Fiorite, o campi immensi, palpitate,
aure marine, nel lunar albor.
Ah...piovete voluttà, volte stellate!
Arde in Tosca un folle amor!

CAVARADOSSI
Ah! M'avvinci ne' tuoi lacci, mia sirena...

TOSCA
Arde a Tosca nel sangue il folle amor!

CAVARADOSSI
Mia sirena, verrò!

TOSCA
Oh, mio amore!

CAVARADOSSI (*Guarda verso la parte d'onde uscì Angelotti.*)
Or lasciami al lavoro.

Do you not long for our little house
that is waiting for us, hidden in the grove?
Our refuge, sacred to us and unseen by the
world,
protected with love and mystery?
Oh, at your side to listen there
to the voices of the night
as they rise through the starlit,
shadowed silences:
from the woods. from the thickets
and the dry grass. from the depths
of shattered tombs
scented with thyme,
the night murmurs
its thousand loves
and false counsels
to soften and seduce the heart.
Oh wide fields, blossom! and sea winds throb
in the moon's radiance, ah,
rain down desire you vaulted stars!
Tosca burns with a mad love!

CAVARADOSSI
Ah! Sorceress, I am bound in your toils...

TOSCA
Tosca's blood burns with a mad love!

CAVARADOSSI
Sorceress, I will come!

TOSCA
Oh, my love!

CAVARADOSSI (*looks towards where Angelotti went out*)
But now you must let me work.

TOSCA
Mi discacci?

CAVARADOSSI
Urge l'opra, lo sai.

TOSCA
Vado! Vado!
(Alza gli occhi e vede il quadro.)
Chi è quella donna bionda lassù?

CAVARADOSSI
La Maddalena. Ti piace?

TOSCA
È troppo bella!

CAVARADOSSI *(ridendo)*
Prezioso elogio!

TOSCA (SOSPETTOSA)
Ridi?
Quegli occhi cilestrini già li vidi...

CAVARADOSSI *(con indifferenza)*
Ce n'è tanti pel mondo!

TOSCA *(cercando ricordare)*
Aspetta...aspetta...
È l'Attavanti!

CAVARADOSSI
Brava!

TOSCA *(cieca di gelosia)*
La vedi? T'ama! Tu l'ami? Tu l'ami?

TOSCA
You dismiss me?

CAVARADOSSI
You know my work is pressing.

TOSCA
I am going!
(Glancing up she sees the painting.)
And who is that blond woman there?

CAVARADOSSI
Mary Magdalene. Do you like her?

TOSCA
She is too beautiful!

CAVARADOSSI *(laughing)*
Ah, rare praise!

TOSCA *(suspicious)*
You laugh?
I have seen those sky-blue eyes before.

CAVARADOSSI *(unconcerned)*
There are so many in the world!

TOSCA *(trying to remember)*
Wait...wait...
Its the young Attavanti!

CAVARADOSSI
Brava!

TOSCA *(blindly jealous)*
Do you see her? She loves you! Do you love her?

CAVARADOSSI
Fu puro caso...

TOSCA
Quei passi e quel bisbiglio...
Ah...Qui stava pur ora!

CAVARADOSSI
Vien via!

TOSCA
Ah, la civetta! A me, a me!

CAVARADOSSI *(serio)*
La vidi ieri, ma fu puro caso...
A pregar qui venne...
Non visto la ritrassi.

TOSCA
Giura!

CAVARADOSSI
Giuro!

TOSCA *(sempre con gli occhi rivolti al quadro)*
Come mi guarda fiso!

CAVARADOSSI
Vien via!

TOSCA
Di me beffarda, ride.

CAVARADOSSI
Follia!
(La tiene presso di sé, fissandola.)

CAVARADOSSI
By pure chance...

TOSCA
Those steps and whispers...
Ah...She was here just now...

CAVARADOSSI
Come here!

TOSCA
The shameless flirt! And to me!

CAVARADOSSI *(serious)*
By pure chance I saw her yesterday...
she came here to pray...
and I, unnoticed, painted her.

TOSCA
Swear!

CAVARADOSSI
I swear!

TOSCA *(her eyes still on the painting)*
How intently she stares at me!

CAVARADOSSI
Come away!

TOSCA
She taunts and mocks me.

CAVARADOSSI
What foolishness!
(holding her close and gazing at her)

TOSCA *(insistente)*
Ah, quegli occhi...

TOSCA *(insisting)*
Ah, those eyes...

CD 1/Track 5   Realizing he will not get rid of Tosca so easily, Mario launches into their famous love duet, musically derived from Tosca's theme music **(02:00)**.

CAVARADOSSI
Quale occhio al mondo può star di paro
all'ardente occhio tuo nero?
È qui che l'esser mio s'affissa intero,
occhio all'amor soave, all'ira fiero...
Qual'altro al mondo può star di paro
all'occhio tuo nero

CAVARADOSSI
What eyes in the world can compare
with your black and glowing eyes?
It is in them that my whole being fastens,
eyes soft with love and rich with anger...
Where in the whole world are eyes
to compare with your black eyes?

TOSCA *(rapita, appoggiando la testa alla spalla di Cavaradossi)*
Oh, come la sai bene
l'arte di farti amare!
(sempre insistendo nella sua idea)
Ma, falle gli occhi neri!

TOSCA *(won over, resting her head or his shoulder)*
Oh, how well you know the art
of capturing women's hearts!
(still persisting in her idea)
But let her eyes be black ones!

CAVARADOSSI
Mia gelosa!

CAVARADOSSI
My jealous Tosca!

TOSCA
Sì, lo sento, ti tormento
senza posa.

TOSCA
Yes, I feel it, I torment you
unceasingly

CAVARADOSSI
Mia gelosa!

CAVARADOSSI
My jealous Tosca!

TOSCA
Certa son del perdono
se tu guardi al mio dolor!

TOSCA
I know you would forgive me
if you knew my grief.

CAVARADOSSI
Mia Tosca idolatrata,
ogni cosa in te mi piace –
l'ira audace
e lo spasimo d'amor!

TOSCA
Dilla ancora,
la parola che consola...
dilla ancora!

CAVARADOSSI
Mia vita, amante inquieta,
dirò sempre, "Floria, t'amo!"
Ah! l'alma acquieta,
sempre "t'amo!" ti dirò!

TOSCA *(sciogliendosi, paurosa d'esser vinta)*
Dio! Quante peccata!
M'hai tutta spettinata.

CAVARADOSSI
Or va, lasciami!

TOSCA
Tu fino a stasera stai fermo al lavoro.
E mi prometti; sia caso o fortuna,
sia treccia bionda o bruna,
a pregar non verrà donna nessuna?

CAVARADOSSI
Lo giuro, amore! Va!

TOSCA
Quanto m'affretti!

CAVARADOSSI
You are my idol, Tosca.
All things in you delight me:
your storming anger
and your pulsing love!

TOSCA
Say again
those consoling words...
Say them again!

CAVARADOSSI
My life, my troubled one, beloved.
I shall always say. "I love you Floria".
Set your uneasy heart at rest,
I shall always say "I love you".

TOSCA *(disengaging, lest she be won completely)*
Good heavens! What a sin!
You have undone my hair.

CAVARADOSSI
Now you must leave me!

TOSCA
You stay at your work until this evening.
And will you promise that, blond locks
or black, by chance or otherwise,
no woman shall come here to pray?

CAVARADOSSI
I swear it beloved. Go now!

TOSCA
How you do hurry me along!

CAVARADOSSI *(con dolce rimprovero, vedendo rispuntare la gelosia)*
Ancora?

CAVARADOSSI *(mildly reproving, as he sees her jealousy returns)*
Come, again?

TOSCA *(cadendo nelle sue braccia e porgendogli la guancia)*
No, perdona!

TOSCA *(falling into his arms, with up-turned cheek)*
No, forgive me!

CAVARADOSSI *(sorridendo)*
Davanti alla Madonna?

CAVARADOSSI *(smiling)*
Before the Madonna?

TOSCA
È tanto buona!...
Ma falle gli occhi neri!

TOSCA
She is so good!
But let her eyes be black ones!

a kiss and Tosca hurries away. Cavaradossi listens to her withdrawing footsteps, then carefully opens the door half-way and peers out. Seeing that all is clear, he runs to the chapel, and Angelotti at once appears from behind the gate.

CAVARADOSSI

CAVARADOSSI

opening the gate for Angelotti, who has naturally heard the foregoing dialogue

È buona la mia Tosca, ma, credente
al confessor, nulla tien celata,
ond'io mi tacqui. È cosa più prudente.

She is good my Tosca, but, as she trusts
her confessor, she hides nothing.
So I must say nothing. It's wiser so.

ANGELOTTI
Siam soli?

ANGELOTTI
Are we alone?

CAVARADOSSI
Sì. Qual è il vostro disegno?

CAVARADOSSI
Yes. What is your plan?

ANGELOTTI
A norma degli eventi, uscir di Stato
o star celato in Roma. Mia sorella...

ANGELOTTI
As things stand now, either to flee the State
or stay in hiding in Rome. My sister...

CAVARADOSSI
L'Attavanti?

ANGELOTTI
Sì; ascose un muliebre
abbigliamento là sotto l'altare,
vesti, velo, ventaglio. Appena imbruni
indosserò quei panni...

CAVARADOSSI
Or comprendo!
Quel fare circospetto
e il pregante fervore
in giovin donna e bella
m'avean messo in sospetto
di qualche occulto amor!
Or comprendo!
Era amor di sorella!

ANGELOTTI
Tutto ella ha osato
onde sottrarmi a Scarpia scellerato!

CAVARADOSSI
Scarpia? Bigotto satiro che affina
colle devote pratiche la foia
libertina e strumento
al lascivo talento
fa il confessore e il boia!
La vita mi costasse, vi salverò!
Ma indugiar fino a notte è mal sicuro.

ANGELOTTI
Temo del sole!

CAVARADOSSI
La cappella mette

CAVARADOSSI
Attavanti?

ANGELOTTI
Yes, she hid some women's clothes
under the altar there,
a dress, a veil, a fan. As soon as it gets dark
I'll put these garments on...

CAVARADOSSI
Now I understand!
That prudent behaviour
and that fervent prayer
in so young and beautiful a woman,
had made me suspect
some secret love!...
Now I understand!
It was the love of a sister!

ANGELOTTI
She has dared all
to save me from that scoundrel Scarpia!

CAVARADOSSI
Scarpia? That licentious bigot who exploits
the uses of religion as refinements
for his libertine lust, and makes
both the confessor and the hangman
the servant of his wantonness!
I'll save you should it cost my life!
But delaying until nightfall is not safe.

ANGELOTTI
I fear the sunlight!

CAVARADOSSI
The chapel gives onto a vegetable garden:

a un orto mal chiuso, poi c'è un canneto
che va lungi pei campi a una mia villa.

ANGELOTTI
M'è nota.

CAVARADOSSI
Ecco la chiave; innanzi sera
io vi raggiungo; portate con voi
le vesti femminili.

ANGELOTTI (*raccoglie in fascio le vestimenta sotto l'altare*)
Ch'io le indossi?

CAVARADOSSI
Per or non monta, il sentier è deserto.

ANGELOTTI (*per uscire*)
Addio!

CAVARADOSSI (*accorrendo verso Angelotti*)
Se urgesse il periglio, correte
al pozzo del giardin. L'acqua è nel fondo,
ma a mezzo della canna, un picciol varco
guida ad un antro oscuro,
rifugio impenetrabile e sicuro!

beyond that is a canefield that winds along
through meadows to my villa.

ANGELOTTI
Yes, I know.

CAVARADOSSI
Here is the key. Before evening
I shall join you there.
Take the woman's costume with you.

ANGELOTTI (*bundling together the clothes from under the altar*)
Should I put them on?

CAVARADOSSI
You needn't now, the path's deserted.

ANGELOTTI (*about to go*)
Good-bye!

CAVARADOSSI (*running towards him*)
If there's sign of danger, go
to the garden well. There's water at the bottom,
but half-way down, a little passage
leads to a dark room. It's a sure,
impenetrable hiding place!

The report of a cannon. The two men look at each other in alarm.

ANGELOTTI
Il cannon del castello!

CAVARADOSSI
Fu scoperta la fuga!
Or Scarpia i suoi sbirri sguinzaglia!

ANGELOTTI
The cannon of the castle!

CAVARADOSSI
They've discovered your escape!
Now Scarpia lets loose his pack of spies!

ANGELOTTI
Addio!

ANGELOTTI
Good-bye!

CAVARADOSSI *(con subita risoluzione)*
Con voi verrò. Staremo all'erta!

CAVARADOSSI *(with sudden resolve)*
I will come with you. We must be on guard!

ANGELOTTI
Odo qualcun!

ANGELOTTI
Someone's coming!

CAVARADOSSI
Se ci assalgon, battaglia!

CAVARADOSSI
If we're attacked we fight!

They leave quickly by the chapel. Enter the sacristan running, bustling and shouting.

SAGRESTANO
Sommo giubilo, Eccellenza!

SACRISTAN
Joyful news, Excellency!

He looks towards the scaffold, and is surprised that once again the painter is not there.

Non c'è più! Ne son dolente!
Chi contrista un miscredente
si guadagna un'indulgenza!

He's gone. I am disappointed.
He who aggrieves a misbeliever
earns an indulgence!

Priests, pupils and singers of the chapel enter tumultuously from every direction.

Tutta qui la cantoria!
Presto!

The whole choir is here!
Hurry!

Other pupils arrive tardily, and at length all group themselves together.

ALLIEVI *(colla massima confusione)*
Dove?

PUPILS *(in great confusion)*
Where?

SAGRESTANO *(spinge alcuni chierici)*
In sagrestia.

SACRISTAN *(pushing some of the priests along)*
In the sacristy.

ALCUNI ALLIEVI
Ma che avvenne?

SAGRESTANO
Nol sapete?
Bonaparte...scellerato...
Bonaparte...

ALTRI
Ebben? Che fu?

SAGRESTANO
Fu spennato, sfracellato
e piombato a Belzebù!

CORO
Chi lo dice? È sogno! È fola!

SAGRESTANO
È veridica parola;
or ne giunse la notizia!

CORO
Si festeggi la vittoria!

SAGRESTANO
E questa sera
gran fiaccolata,
veglia di gala a Palazzo Farnese,
ed un'apposita nuova cantata
con Floria Tosca!
E nelle chiese
inni al Signor!
Or via a vestirvi,
non più clamor!
Via, via in sagrestia!

SOME PUPILS
But what's happened?

SACRISTAN
You haven't heard?
Bonaparte...the scoundrel...
Bonaparte...

OTHERS
Well? What?

SACRISTAN
He was plucked and quartered
and thrown to Beelzebub!

CHORUS
Who says so? It's a dream! It's nonsense!

SACRISTAN
Its a true report.
The news just reached us.

CHORUS
Let's celebrate the victory!

SACRISTAN
And tonight
a mighty torch procession,
a gala evening at Farnese Palace,
and a new cantata for the great occasion
with Flora Tosca!
And in the churches,
hymns to the Lord!
Now get along and dress,
and no more shouting.
On with you to the sacristy!

CORO *(ridendo et gridando)*	**CHORUS** *(laughing and shouting gaily)*
Veglia di gala,	Double pay...Te Deum...Gloria!
si festeggi la vittoria! ecc.	Long live the King! Let's celebrate the
	victory! etc.

Their shouting is at its height when an ironic voice cuts short the uproar of songs and laughter. It is Scarpia. Behind him, Spoletta and several policemen

CD 1/Track 7   Again we hear Scarpia's theme in the full orchestra as he enters and the mood of celebration suddenly becomes one of fear.

SCARPIA	**SCARPIA**
Un tal baccano in chiesa!	Such a hubbub in church!
Bel rispetto!	A fine respect!
SAGRESTANO *(balbettando impaurito)*	**SACRISTAN** *(stammering with fright)*
Eccellenza, il gran giubilo...	Excellency, the joyous news...
SCARPIA	**SCARPIA**
Apprestate per il Te Deum.	Prepare for the Te Deum.

All depart crest-fallen; even the sacristan hopes to slip away, but Scarpia brusquely detains him.

Tu resta.	You stay here!
SAGRESTANO *(impaurito)*	**SACRISTAN** *(cowering)*
Non mi muovo!	I shan't move!
SCARPIA *(a Spoletta)*	**SCARPIA** *(to Spoletta)*
E tu va, fruga ogni angolo, raccogli	And you search every corner,
ogni traccia.	track down every clue.
SPOLETTA	**SPOLETTA**
Sta bene!	Very well.

SCARPIA *(ad altri sbirri)*
Occhio alle porte,
senza dar sospetti!
(al sagrestano)
Ora a te...
Pesa le tue risposte.
Un prigionier di Stato
fuggì pur ora da Castel Sant'Angelo...
S'è rifugiato qui.

SAGRESTANO
Misericordia!

SCARPIA
Forse c'è ancora. Dov'è la cappella
degli Attavanti?

SAGRESTANO
Eccola.

goes to the gate and finds it half-open

Aperta! Arcangeli!
E un'altra chiave!

SCARPIA
Buon indizio. Entriamo.

They enter the chapel and then return. Scarpia, balked, has a fan in his hands which he shakes nervously.

Fu grave sbaglio
quel colpo di cannone! Il mariolo
spiccato ha il volo, ma lasciò una preda
preziosa, un ventaglio.
Qual complice il misfatto
preparò?

SCARPIA *(to other policemen)*
Keep watch at the doors,
Without arousing suspicion!
(to sacristan)
Now, as for you...
weigh your answers well.
A prisoner of State
has just escaped from Castel Sant'Angelo.
He took refuge here.

SACRISTAN
Heaven help us!

SCARPIA
He may still be here.
Where is the chapel of the Attavanti?

SACRISTAN
That is it there.

It's open...Merciful Heaven!
And there's another key!

SCARPIA
A good sign. Let's go in.

It was a bad mistake
to fire the cannon. The cheat
has flown the roost, but left behind
a precious clue, a fan.
Who was the accomplice
in his flight?

He puzzles over the situation, then examines the fan; suddenly notices the coat of arms.

La Marchesa Attavanti! Il suo stemma...	The Marchesa Attavanti! Its her crest...

looks around scrutinising every corner of the church. His gaze rests on the scaffold, the painter's tools, the painting...and he recognises the familiar features of the Attavanti in the face of the saint.

Il suo ritratto!	Her portrait!
(al sagrestano)	*(to the sacristan)*
Chi fe' quelle pitture?	Who painted that picture?

SAGRESTANO	**SACRISTAN**
Il cavalier Cavaradossi.	The Cavalier Cavaradossi.

SCARPIA	**SCARPIA**
Lui!	He!

One of the policemen returns from the chapel bringing the basket which Cavaradossi gave to Angelotti.

SAGRESTANO	**SACRISTAN**
Numi! Il paniere!	Heavens! The basket!

SCARPIA *(seguitando le sue riflessioni)*	**SCARPIA** *(pursuing his own thoughts)*
Lui! L'amante di Tosca! Un uom sospetto!	He! Tosca's lover! A suspect character!
Un volterrian!	A revolutionary!

SAGRESTANO *(che andò a guardare il paniere)*	**SACRISTAN** *(peering into the basket)*
Vuoto! Vuoto!	Empty! Empty!

SCARPIA	**SCARPIA**
Che hai detto?	What do you say?
(Vede lo sbirro col paniere.)	*(on seeing the policeman with the basket)*
Che fu?	What's that?

SAGRESTANO *(prendendo il paniere)*
Si ritrovò nella cappella
questo panier.

SCARPIA
Tu lo conosci?

SAGRESTANO
Certo!
(esitante e pauroso)
È il cesto del pittor...ma...nondimeno...

SCARPIA
Sputa quello che sai.

SAGRESTANO
Io lo lasciai ripieno
di cibo prelibato...
Il pranzo del pittor!

SCARPIA *(attento, inquirente per scoprir terreno)*
Avrà pranzato!

SAGRESTANO
Nella cappella? Non ne avea la chiave,
né contava pranzar, disse egli stesso.
Ond'io l'avea già messo al riparo.
Libera me Domine!

He shows where he put the basket, and leaves it there.

SCARPIA *(fra sé)*
Or tutto è chiaro...
La provvista del sacrista
d'Angelotti fu la preda!

He sees Tosca, who enters in haste.

SACRISTAN *(taking the basket)*
They found this basket
in the chapel.

SCARPIA
Have you seen it before?

SACRISTAN
Yes, indeed!
(hesitant and fearful)
It's the painter's basket...but...even so...

SCARPIA
Spit out what you know!

SACRISTAN
I left it for him filled
with excellent food...
The painter's meal!

SCARPIA *(attentive, seeking to discover more)*
Then he must have eaten!

SACRISTAN
In the chapel? No. He had no key,
nor did he want to eat. He told me so himself.
So I put the basket safely to one side.
Libera me domine!

SCARPIA *(to himself)*
It's all clear now...
The sacristan's food
became Angelotti's booty!

Tosca? Che non mi veda.

Tosca? She must not see me.

He hides behind the column with the basin of Holy Water.

Per ridurre un geloso allo sbaraglio
Jago ebbe un fazzoletto, ed io un ventaglio!

Iago had a handkerchief, and I a fan
to drive a jealous lover to distraction!

TOSCA

TOSCA

runs towards the scaffold sure of finding Cavaradossi, and is taken aback or not seeing him there

Mario! Mario!

Mario! Mario!

SAGRESTANO *(che si trova ai piedi dell'impalco)*
Il pittor Cavaradossi?
Chi sa dove sia?

SACRISTAN *(at the foot of the scaffold)*
The painter Cavaradossi?
Who knows where the heretic is; and with whom?

Svanì, sgattaiolò
per sua stregoneria.

He's slipped away, evaporated
by his own witchcraft.

He slips away.

TOSCA
Ingannata? No, no...
Tradirmi egli non può!

TOSCA
Deceived? No...
He could not betray me!

SCARPIA

SCARPIA

circling the column, he advances towards the astonished Tosca. Dips his finger in the basin, and offers her the Holy Water. Bells sound outside, summoning the faithful to the church.

Tosca divina,
la mano mia
la vostra aspetta, piccola manina,
non per galanteria
ma per offrirvi l'acqua benedetta.

Divine Tosca,
my hand awaits
your delicate hand.
Not out of idle gallantry
but to offer Holy Water.

TOSCA

TOSCA

touching Scarpias hand and crossing herself

Grazie, Signor!

Thank you, Sir!

Slowly the central nave of the church fills with the faithful-people of every station, rich and poor, townsmen and peasants, soldiers and beggars. Then a cardinal, with the head of the convent, proceeds to the main altar. Before that altar, the crowd jams into the central nave.

SCARPIA
Un nobile
esempio è il vostro; al cielo
piena di santo zelo
attingete dell'arte il magistero
che la fede ravviva!

SCARPIA
It is a noble example
that you give, Tosca;
filled with holy zeal, you draw
from Heaven the mastery of art
to revive the faith of men.

TOSCA *(distratta e pensosa)*
Bontà vostra.

TOSCA *(distraught and preoccupied)*
You are too kind.

SCARPIA
Le pie donne son rare...
Voi calcate la scena...
(con intenzione)
e in chiesa ci venite per pregar.

SCARPIA
Pious women are so rare...
Your life's the stage...
(significantly)
Yet you come to church to pray.

TOSCA *(sorpresa)*
Che intendete?

TOSCA *(surprised)*
What do you mean?

SCARPIA
E non fate
come certe sfrontate

SCARPIA
And you are not
as other strumpets are

points to the portrait

che han di Maddalena
viso e costumi...e vi trescan d'amore!
℃ 78

who have the dress and face of Magdalene
and come to scheme in love.

TOSCA *(scatta pronta)*
Che? D'amore? Le prove!

SCARPIA *(mostra il ventaglio)*
È arnese di pittore questo?

TOSCA *(lo afferra)*
Un ventaglio! Dove stava?

SCARPIA
Là su quel palco. Qualcun venne
certo a sturbar gli amanti
ed essa nel fuggir perdé le penne!

TOSCA *(esaminando il ventaglio)*
La corona! Lo stemma! È l'Attavanti!
Presago sospetto!

TOSCA *(at once aroused)*
What? In love? Your proof?

SCARPIA *(showing her the fan)*
Is this a painter's tool?

TOSCA *(grabbing it)*
A fan! Where was it?

SCARPIA
There on the scaffold. Obviously
somebody surprised the lovers,
and she lost her feathers in her flight!

TOSCA *(studying the fan)*
The crown! The crest! Its the Attavanti's!
Oh prophetic doubt!

CD 1/Track 8 To the incongruous accompaniment of church bells, **(00:54)** Scarpia begins to work out his evil plan to seduce Tosca and bring her lover to justice.

SCARPIA *(fra sé)*
Ho sortito l'effetto!

TOSCA

SCARPIA *(to himself)*
I've hit the mark!

TOSCA

forgetting both the place and Scarpia, tries to hold back her tears

Ed io venivo a lui tutta dogliosa
per dirgli; invan stasera, il ciel s'infosca,
l'innamorata Tosca è prigioniera...

And I came sadly here to tell him
that in vain, tonight, the sky will darken:
for the lovesick Tosca is a prisoner...

SCARPIA *(fra sé)*
Già il veleno l'ha rosa!

TOSCA
Dei regali tripudi, prigioniera!

SCARPIA *(to himself)*
The poison bites home already!

TOSCA
...A prisoner of the royal jubilee!

79

SCARPIA (fra sé)
Già il veleno l'ha rosa!
(mellifluo a Tosca)
O che v'offende,
dolce Signora?
Una ribelle
lagrima scende
sovra le belle
guancie e le irrora;
dolce Signora,
che m'ai v'accora?

TOSCA
Nulla!

SCARPIA (insinuante)
Darei la vita
per asciugar quel pianto.

TOSCA (non ascoltandolo)
Io qui mi struggo e intanto
d'altra in braccio le mie smanie deride!

SCARPIA (fra sé)
Morde il veleno!

TOSCA (sempre più crucciosa)
Dove son? Potessi
coglierli, i traditori. Oh qual sospetto!
Ai doppi amori
è la villa ricetto!
Traditor! Traditor!
(con immenso dolore)
Oh mio bel nido insozzato di fango!
(con pronta risoluzione)
Vi piomberò inattesa.

SCARPIA (to himself)
The poison bites home already!
(sweetly to Tosca)
Oh gracious lady,
what avails you?
For I see
a rebel tear
mars your fair cheek
and moistens it.
Oh gracious lady,
why are you grieving?

TOSCA
It is nothing!

SCARPIA (insinuating)
I would give my life
to wipe away those tears.

TOSCA (unheeding)
Here I am heartbroken, while he
in another's arms, mocks at my anguish.

SCARPIA (to himself)
The poison bites deep.

TOSCA (her anger rising)
Where are they? Could I but catch
the traitors! Oh dark suspicion!
Double loves now nest
inside this villa!
Oh traitor!
(with immense grief)
Oh my fair nest befouled with mud!
(with quick resolve)
I'll fall upon them unexpected!

turns threateningly towards the portrait

Tu non l'avrai stasera. Giuro!	You shall not have him tonight, I swear!

SCARPIA *(scandalizzato, quasi rimproverandola)*
In chiesa!

SCARPIA *(with a scandalised air and tone of rebuke)*
In church!

TOSCA
Dio mio perdona. Egli vede ch'io piango!

TOSCA
God will pardon me. He sees me weeping!

She leaves in great distress, Scarpia accompanying her and pretending to reassure her. As she leaves, he returns to the column and makes a sign.

CD 1/Track 10 This is one of the most chilling scenes in all of opera. Again the church bells call worshippers to the celebration. As they gather in prayer, Scarpia pours out his lust for Tosca, saying finally that she makes him forget God. He turns and joins in the assembly's prayer, and the act closes as it began, with the villain's theme blaring in the orchestra.

SCARPIA *(a Spoletta che sbuca di dietro la colonna)*
Tre sbirri, una carrozza...Presto, seguila dovunque vada, non visto. Provvedi!

SCARPIA *(to Spoletta, who emerges from behind the column)*
Three men and a carriage...Quick, follow Wherever she goes! And take care!

SPOLETTA
Sta bene. Il convegno?

SPOLETTA
Yes Sir. And where do we meet?

SCARPIA
Palazzo Farnese!

SCARPIA
Farnese Palace!

Spoletta hurries out with three policemen.

Va, Tosca!
Nel tuo cuor s'annida Scarpia!...
Va, Tosca! È Scarpia che scioglie a volo
il falco della tua gelosia.
Quanta promessa nel tuo pronto sospetto!

Go, Tosca!
Now Scarpia digs a nest within your heart!
Go, Tosca!. Scarpia now sets loose
the soaring falcon of your jealousy!
How great a promise in your quick suspicions!

Nel tuo cuor s'annida Scarpia!...
Va, Tosca!

Now Scarpia digs a nest within your heart!
Go, Tosca!

Scarpia kneels and prays as the cardinal passes.

CORO
Adjutorum nostrum in nomine Domini
qui fecit coelum et terram.
Sit nomen Domini benedictum
et hoc nunc et usque in saeculum.

CHORUS
Adjutorum nostrum in nomine Domini
qui fecit coelum et terram.
Sit nomen Domini benedictum
et hoc nunc et usque in speculum.

SCARPIA
A doppia mira tendo il voler,
né il capo del ribelle è la più preziosa...
Ah di quegli occhi vittoriosi veder la
fiamma illanguidir
con spasimo d'amor fra le mie braccia
illanguidir d'amor...
l'uno al capestro,
l'altra fra le mie braccia...

SCARPIA
My will takes aim now at a double target,
nor is the rebel's head the bigger prize...
Ah, to see the flame of those imperious
eyes
grow faint and languid with passion...

For him, the rope,
and for her. my arms...

CORO
Te Deum laudamus:
Te Deum confitemur!

CHORUS
Te Deum laudamus:
Te Deum confitemur!

The sacred chant from the back of the church startles Scarpia, as though awakening him from a dream. He collects himself, makes the Sign of the Cross.

SCARPIA
Tosca, mi fai dimenticare Iddio!...

SCARPIA
Tosca you make me forget God!

He kneels and prays devoutly.

CORO, SCARPIA
Te aeternum
patrem omnis terra veneratur!

CHORUS, SCARPIA
Te aeturnum
Patrem omnis terra veneratur!

Act 2

SCARPIA'S APARTMENT ON AN UPPER FLOOR OF THE FARNESE PALACE

(A table set for supper. A wide window opening on the palace courtyard. It is night. Scarpia is at the table taking his supper; every now and again he pauses to reflect. He looks at his watch; he is angry and preoccupied.)

CD 2/Track 1   The curtain opens immediately and we hear a casual descending motive in the orchestra as Scarpia sits down to dinner.

SCARPIA
Tosca è un buon falco!
Certo a quest'ora
i miei segugi le due prede azzannano!
Doman sul palco
vedrà l'aurora
Angelotti e il bel Mario al laccio pendere.

SCARPIA
Tosca is a good falcon!
Surely by this time
my hounds have fallen on their double prey!
And tomorrow's dawn will see
Angelotti on the scaffold
and the fine Mario hanging from a noose.

He rings a bell. Enter Sciarrone.

Tosca è a Palazzo?

Is Tosca in the palace?

SCIARRONE
Un ciambellan ne uscia
pur ora in traccia.

SCIARRONE
A chamberlain has just gone
to look for her.

SCARPIA *(accenna la finestra)*
Apri. Tarda è la notte.

SCARPIA *(points towards the window)*
Open the window. It is late.

The sound of an orchestra is heard from the lower floor, where Maria Carolina, the Queen of Naples, is giving a party in honour of Melas.

Alla cantata ancor manca la Diva.	The Diva's still missing from the concert.
E strimpellan gavotte.	And they strum gavottes.

to Sciarrone

Tu attenderai la Tosca in sull'entrata.	Wait for Tosca at the entrance:
Le dirai ch'io l'aspetto	tell her I shall expect her
finita la cantata...	after the concert.
O meglio...	Or better...

rises and goes to write a note

Le darai questo biglietto.	Give her this note.

Exit Sciarrone. Scarpia resumes his seat at the table.

Ella verrà per amor del suo Mario!	She will come for love of her Mario!
Per amor del suo Mario al piacer mio	And for love of Mario she will yield
s'arrenderà. Tal dei profondi amori	to my pleasure. Such is the profound mis-
è la profonda miseria.	ery of profound love...

CD 2/Track 2   Puccini rarely wrote arias for his baritone characters, but this is one of his great-est. Scarpia reflects on how he was made for power and lust. The piece owes much in character and content to Iago's famous Credo in Verdi's Otello.

Ha più forte	For myself the violent conquest
sapore la conquista violenta	has stronger relish than the soft surrender.
che il mellifluo consenso. Io di sospiri	I take no delight in sighs or vows
e di lattiginose albe lunari	exchanged at misty lunar dawn.
poco mi appago. Non so trarre accordi	I know not how to draw
di chitarra, né oròscopo di fior	harmony from guitars, or horoscopes,
né far l'occhio di pesce, o tubar come	from flowers. nor am I apt at dalliance,
tortora! Bramo. La cosa bramata	or cooing like the turtle dove. I crave,

perseguo, me ne sazio e via la getto.
Volto a nuova esca. Dio creò diverse
beltà e vini diversi. Io vo' gustar
quanto più posso dell'opra divina!

I pursue the craved thing, sate myself and
cast it by,
and seek new bait. God made diverse
beauties
as he made diverse wines, and of these
God-like works I mean to taste my full.

He drinks. Enter Sciarrone.

SCIARRONE
Spoletta è giunto.

SCIARRONE
Spoletta's here.

SCARPIA
Entri. In buon punto.

SCARPIA
Show him in. In good time, too.

Enter Spoletta. Scarpia questions him without looking up from his supper.

O galantuomo, come andò la caccia?

Well, my fine man, how did the hunt go?

SPOLETTA *(a parte)*
Sant'Ignazio mi aiuta!

SPOLETTA *(aside)*
Saint Ignatius help me!

to Scarpia

Della signora seguimmo la traccia.
Giunti a un'erma villetta
tra le fratte perduta,
ella vi entrò. Ne uscì sola ben presto.
Allor scavalco lesto
il muro del giardin coi miei cagnotti
e piombo in casa...

We kept on the lady's trail
following her to a lonely villa
lost in the woods.
She entered there and soon came out alone.
At once with my dogs I vaulted over
the garden wall and
burst into the house.

SCARPIA
Quel bravo Spoletta!

SCARPIA
Well done, Spoletta!

SPOLETTA
Fiuto! razzolo! frugo!

SPOLETTA
I sniff...I scratch...I rummage

SCARPIA (*si avvede dell'indecisione di Spoletta e si leva ritto, pallido d'ira, le ciglia corrugate*)
Ahi! L'Angelotti?

SCARPIA (*sensing Spoletta's hesitation, rises scowling and pale with anger*)
And Angelotti?

SPOLETTA
Non s'è trovato.

SPOLETTA
Nowhere to be found.

SCARPIA (*furente*)
Ah cane! Ah traditore!
Ceffo di basilisco,
alle forche!

SCARPIA (*in a rage*)
Ah dog! Traitor!
Snout of a snake.
To the gallows!

SPOLETTA
Gesù!

SPOLETTA
Jesus!

trying to appease Scarpia's wrath

C'era il pittore...

The painter was there...

SCARPIA
Cavaradossi?

SCARPIA
Cavaradossi?

SPOLETTA (*accenna di sì, ed aggiunge pronto:*)
Ei sa dove l'altro s'asconde.
Ogni suo gesto, ogni accento, tradìa
tal beffarda ironia,
ch'io lo trassi in arresto!

SPOLETTA (*nods and quickly adds*)
And he knows where the other is.
He showed such taunting irony
in every word and gesture
that I arrested him.

SCARPIA (*con sospiro di soddisfazione*)
Meno male!

SCARPIA (*with a sigh of satisfaction*)
Not bad, not bad.

SPOLETTA (*accenna all'anticamera*)
Egli è là.

SPOLETTA (*waving towards the antechamber*)
He is there.

Scarpia paces up and down, pondering. He stops abruptly as he hears, through the open window, the choral cantata being sung in the Queen's apartment.

SCARPIA *(a Spoletta)*
Introducete il Cavaliere.

SCARPIA *(to Spoletta)*
Bring in the Cavalier.

Exit Spoletta. To Sciarrone

A me Roberti e Il Giudice del Fisco.

Fetch Roberti and the judge.

Exit Sciarrone. Scarpia sits down again. Spoletta and four bailiffs bring in Mario Cavaradossi; then enter Roberti the executioner, the judge with a scribe, and Sciarrone.

CAVARADOSSI *(alteramente)*
Tal violenza!

CAVARADOSSI *(with disdain)*
Such violence.

SCARPIA *(con studiata cortesia)*
Cavalier, vi piaccia accomodarvi.

SCARPIA *(with studied courtesy)*
Cavalier, please be seated.

CAVARADOSSI
Vo' saper...

CAVARADOSSI
I want to know...

SCARPIA

SCARPIA

indicating a chair at the other side of the table

Sedete.

Be seated.

CAVARADOSSI *(rifiutando)*
Aspetto.

CAVARADOSSI *(declining)*
I'll stand.

SCARPIA
E sia. Vi è noto che un prigione...

SCARPIA
As you wish. Are you aware that a prisoner...

Tosca's voice is heard in the cantata.

CAVARADOSSI
La sua voce!

CAVARADOSSI
Her voice!

SCARPIA

who has paused on hearing Tosca's voice

Vi è noto che un prigione
oggi è fuggito da Castel Sant'Angelo?

CAVARADOSSI
Ignoro.

SCARPIA
Eppur, si pretende che voi
l'abbiate accolto in Sant'Andrea, provvisto
di cibo, di vesti...

CAVARADOSSI *(risoluto)*
Menzogna!

SCARPIA *(continuando a mantenersi calmo)*
...e guidato
ad un vostro podere suburbano.

CAVARADOSSI
Nego. Le prove?

SCARPIA *(mellifluo)*
Un suddito fedele...

CAVARADOSSI
Al fatto. Chi mi accusa? I vostri birri
invan frugar la villa.

SCARPIA
Segno che è ben celata.

CAVARADOSSI
Sospetti di spia!

SCARPIA

SCARPIA

You are aware that a prisoner
fled today from Sant'Angelo Castle?

CAVARADOSSI
I did not know it.

SCARPIA
And yet it's reported
that you sheltered him in Sant'Andrea.
Gave him food and clothing...

CAVARADOSSI *(unflinching)*
Lies.

SCARPIA *(still quite calm)*
...and took him
to a suburban place of yours.

CAVARADOSSI
I deny that. What proof have you?

SCARPIA *(sweetly)*
A faithful servant...

CAVARADOSSI
The facts! Who's my accuser? In vain
your spies ransacked my villa.

SCARPIA
Proof that he is hidden well.

CAVARADOSSI
Suspicions of a spy!

SPOLETTA *(offeso)*
Alle nostre ricerche egli rideva...

CAVARADOSSI
E rido ancor. E rido ancor.

SCARPIA *(con accento severo)*
Questo è luogo di lacrime! Badate!
Or basta! Rispondete!

He rises and angrily shuts the window to be undisturbed by the singing from the floor below, then turns imperiously to Cavaradossi.

Ov'è Angelotti?

CAVARADOSSI
Non lo so.

SCARPIA
Negate avergli dato cibo?

CAVARADOSSI
Nego!

SCARPIA
E vesti?

CAVARADOSSI
Nego!

SCARPIA
Ed asilo nella villa?
E che là sia nascosto?

CAVARADOSSI *(con forza)*
Nego! Nego!

SPOLETTA *(offended)*
He laughed at our questions...

CAVARADOSSI
And I laugh still!

SCARPIA *(harshly)*
Beware! This is a place for tears!
Enough now. Answer me!

Where is Angelotti?

CAVARADOSSI
I don't know.

SCARPIA
You deny you gave him food?

CAVARADOSSI
I deny it.

SCARPIA
And clothes?

CAVARADOSSI
I deny it.

SCARPIA
And refuge in your villa?
And that he's hidden there?

CAVARADOSSI *(vehemently)*
I deny it! I deny it!

SCARPIA *(astutamente, ritornando calmo)*
Via, Cavaliere, riflettete:
saggia non è cotesta ostinatezza vostra.
Angoscia grande, pronta confessione eviterà!
Io vi consiglio, dite:
Dov'è dunque Angelotti?

CAVARADOSSI
Non lo so.

SCARPIA
Ancor l'ultima volta. Dov'è?

CAVARADOSSI
Nol so!

SPOLETTA *(fra sé)*
O bei tratti di corda!

Enter Tosca breathless.

SCARPIA *(fra sé)*
Eccola!

TOSCA *(vede Cavaradossi e corre ad abbracciarlo)*
Mario, tu qui?

CAVARADOSSI *(sommessamente)*
Di quanto là vedesti, taci,
o m'uccidi!

Tosca indicates she understands.

SCARPIA *(con solennità)*
Mario Cavaradossi,
qual testimone il Giudice vi aspetta.
(a Roberti)

SCARPIA *(craftily, becoming calm)*
Come, Cavalier, you must reflect.
This stubbornness of yours is not prudent.
A prompt confession saves enormous pain.
Take my advice and tell me:
where is Angelotti?

CAVARADOSSI
I don't know.

SCARPIA
Be careful. For the last time. where is he?

CAVARADOSSI
I don't know.

SPOLETTA *(to himself)*
Oh, for a good whipping!

SCARPIA *(to himself)*
Here she is!

TOSCA *(sees Cavaradossi and runs to embrace him)*
Mario, you. here?

CAVARADOSSI *(speaking low)*
Of what you saw there, say nothing.
Or you will kill me!

SCARPIA *(solemnly)*
Mario Cavaradossi,
the judge awaits your testimony.
(to Roberti)

Pria le forme ordinarie.	First, the usual formalities.
Indi...ai miei cenni.	And then...as I shall order.

Sciarrone opens the door to the torture chamber. The judge goes in and the others follow. Spoletta stations himself at the door at the back of the room. Tosca and Scarpia are now alone together.

CD 2/Track 5   The orchestra opens this scene with a theme representing suffering, which gives way to a theme that binds much of the act together, the theme associated with torture **(02:54)**.

SCARPIA	**SCARPIA**
Ed or fra noi parliam da buoni amici.	And now let's talk together like good friends.
Via quell'aria sgomentata.	Come now. don't look so frightened.
TOSCA *(con calma studiata)*	**TOSCA** *(with studied calm)*
Sgomento alcun non ho.	I am not afraid.
SCARPIA	**SCARPIA**
La storia del ventaglio?	What about the fan?

passes behind the sofa where Tosca is sitting and leans upon it. He still adopts a gallant air.

TOSCA *(con simulata indifferenza)*	**TOSCA** *(with feigned indifference)*
Fu sciocca gelosia.	That was foolish jealousy.
SCARPIA	**SCARPIA**
L'Attavanti non era dunque alla villa?	So, the Attavanti was not at the villa?
TOSCA	**TOSCA**
No, egli era solo.	No, he was alone.
SCARPIA	**SCARPIA**
Solo? Ne siete ben sicura?	Alone? Are you quite sure?

TOSCA
Nulla sfugge ai gelosi. Solo! Solo!

SCARPIA

taking a chair he places it in front of Tosca, sits down, and studies her face

Davver?

TOSCA *(irritata)*
Solo, sì!

SCARPIA
Quanto fuoco! Par che abbiate paura
di tradirvi.
(a Sciarrone)
Sciarrone, che dice il Cavalier?

SCIARRONE *(apparendo)*
Nega.

SCARPIA

raising his voice, towards the open door

Insistiamo.

Sciarrone goes out and shuts the door.

TOSCA *(ridendo)*
Oh, è inutil!

SCARPIA *(serio, passeggiando)*
Lo vedremo, signora.

TOSCA
Dunque per compiacervi si dovrebbe mentir?

TOSCA
Nothing escapes a jealous eye. Alone. Alone.

SCARPIA

Indeed!

TOSCA *(annoyed)*
Yes. Alone!

SCARPIA
You protest too much! Perhaps you fear
you may betray yourself.
(to Sciarrone)
Sciarrone, what does the Cavalier have to say?

SCIARRONE *(appearing)*
He denies everything.

SCARPIA

Keep pressing him!

TOSCA *(laughing}*
You know it's quite useless.

SCARPIA *(serious. pacing back and forth)*
We shall see, Madam.

TOSCA
It seems that one must lie to please you?

SCARPIA
No, ma il vero potrebbe abbreviargli un ora
assai penosa...

TOSCA *(sorpresa)*
Un'ora penosa? Che vuol dir?
Che avviene in quella stanza?

SCARPIA
È forza che si adempia la legge.

TOSCA
Oh, Dio! Che avvien, che avvien, che
avvien?...

SCARPIA
Legato mani e piè il vostro amante
ha un cerchio uncinato alle tempia
che ad ogni niego ne sprizza sangue senza
mercé!

TOSCA *(balza in piedi)*
Non è ver, non è ver!
Sogghigno di demone!

a prolonged groan from Cavaradossi

Un gemito? Pietà...pietà!...

SCARPIA
Sta in voi di salvarlo.

TOSCA
Ebben, ma cessate, cessate!

SCARPIA
No, but the truth might shorten
an extremely painful hour for him...

TOSCA *(surprised)*
A painful hour? What do you mean?
What are you doing in that room?

SCARPIA
It is force that carries out the law.

TOSCA
Oh, God! What's happening? What is
happening?

SCARPIA
Your lover's bound hand and foot.
A ring of hooked iron at his temples.
So that they spurt blood at each denial.

TOSCA *(bounds to her feet)*
It isn't true! It isn't true!
Oh, leering devil!

He groans! Oh, pity! Pity!

SCARPIA
It is up to you to save him.

TOSCA
Good, good! But stop it! Stop it!

SCARPIA *(gridando)*
Sciarrone, sciogliete.

SCARPIA *(shouting)*
Stop it, Sciarrone!

SCIARRONE *(appare)*
Tutto?

SCIARRONE *(appearing)*
Stop everything?

SCARPIA
Tutto.

SCARPIA
Everything.

Sciarrone returns to the torture chamber, shutting the door.

Ed or, la verità!

And now the truth!

TOSCA
Ch'io lo veda!

TOSCA
Let me see him.

SCARPIA
No!

SCARPIA
No!

TOSCA *(riesce ad avvicinarsi all'uscio)*
Mario!

TOSCA *(managing to get near the door)*
Mario!

LA VOCE DI CAVARADOSSI
Tosca!

CAVARADOSSI'S VOICE
Tosca!

TOSCA
Ti straziano ancora?

TOSCA
Are they still! torturing you?

LA VOCE DI CAVARADOSSI
No, coraggio! Taci, sprezzo il dolor!

CAVARADOSSI'S VOICE
No. Courage...and be silent. I despise pain!

SCARPIA
6   Orsù, Tosca parlate.

SCARPIA
Come on Tosca, speak!

TOSCA *(rinfrancata dalle parole di Mario)*
Non so nulla!

TOSCA *(strengthened by Mario's words)*
I know nothing.

SCARPIA
Non vale quella prova?
Roberti, ripigliamo...

TOSCA

throwing herself in front of the door, to keep him from giving the order

No! Fermate!

SCARPIA
Voi parlerete?

TOSCA
No, no! Ah!...mostro...
Lo strazi, lo uccidi!

SCARPIA
Lo strazia quel vostro
silenzio assai più.

TOSCA
Tu ridi
all'orrida pena?

SCARPIA *(con feroce ironia)*
Mai Tosca alla scena
più tragica fu!
(a Spoletta)
Aprite le porte
che n'oda i lamenti

Spoletta opens the door and stands stiffly on the threshold.

LA VOCE DI CAVARADOSSI
Vi sfido!

SCARPIA
Wasn't that enough for you?
Roberti, start again...

TOSCA

No! Stop!

SCARPIA
Will you speak?

TOSCA
No, no! Ah, monster!
Murderer...you're killing him!

SCARPIA
It's your silence
that's killing him.

TOSCA
Monster, do you laugh
at this ghastly torment?

SCARPIA *(with fierce irony)*
Tosca on the stage
was never more tragic!
(to Spoletta)
Open the door so she
can hear his groans better.

CAVARADOSSI'S VOICE
I defy you.

SCARPIA
Più forte! Più forte!...

LA VOCE DI CAVARADOSSI
Vi sfido!

SCARPIA (a Tosca)
Parlate...

TOSCA
Che dire?

SCARPIA
Su, via...

TOSCA
Ah, non so nulla! Ah!
Dovrei mentir?

SCARPIA
Dite, dov'è Angelotti?

TOSCA
No! No!

SCARPIA
Parlate su, via, dove celato sta?
Su via, parlate, ov'è?

TOSCA
Più non posso! Ah! Che orror!
Cessate il martir!...È troppo soffrir...
Non posso più...non posso più!

LA VOCE DI CAVARADOSSI
Ahime!

SCARPIA
Harder! Harder!

CAVARADOSSI'S VOICE
I defy you all!

SCARPIA (to Tosca)
Speak now...

TOSCA
What can I say?

SCARPIA
Come, speak...

TOSCA
Oh, I know nothing!
Must I lie to you?

SCARPIA
Where's Angelotti?

TOSCA
No, no!

SCARPIA
Speak up, come, quickly.
Where's he hiding?

TOSCA
I can stand no more. Oh, horror!
Stop this torture...It's more than I can bear...
I can stand no more...no more...

CAVARADOSSI'S VOICE
Ah!

TOSCA

TOSCA

she turns imploringly to Scarpia, who signals to Spoletta to let her come near; she goes to the open door and is overwhelmed by the horrible scene within. She cries out in anguish to Cavaradossi.

Mario, consenti ch'io parli?

Mario, will you let me speak?

LA VOCE DI CAVARADOSSI
No. No.

CAVARADOSSI'S VOICE
No.

TOSCA *(con insistenza)*
Ascolta, non posso più...

TOSCA *(pleading)*
Listen, I can bear no more...

LA VOCE DI CAVARADOSSI
Stolta, che sai? Che puoi dir?

CAVARADOSSI'S VOICE
Fool! What do you know and what can you say?

SCARPIA *(irritatissimo per le parole di Cavaradossi, grida terribile a Spoletta:)*
Ma fatelo tacere!

SCARPIA *(enraged at this, shouts furiously at Spoletta)*
Shut him up!

Spoletta goes into the torture chamber, returning after a moment. Tosca overcome with emotion, has fallen prostrate on the sofa. Sobbing she appeals to Scarpia. He stands silent and impassive. Spoletta, meanwhile, mumbles a prayer under his breath: Judex ergo cum sedebit quidquid latet apparebit nil inultum remanebit.

TOSCA
Che v'ho fatto in vita mia? Son io
che così torturate! Torturate
l'anima...

TOSCA
What have I done to you in my life?
It is I you torture so.
It is my spirit...

bursts into convulsive sobs

Sì, l'anima mi torturate!

Yes, my spirit you are torturing.

SPOLETTA *(continua a pregare:)*
Nil inultum remanebit!

SPOLETTA *(continues to pray)*
Nil inultum remanebit!

Scarpia profiting from Tosca's breakdown goes towards the torture chamber and orders the resumption of the torment. There is a piercing cry, Tosca leaps up, and in a choking voice says rapidly to Scarpia:

TOSCA
Nel pozzo...nel giardino...

TOSCA
In the well, in the garden...

SCARPIA
Là è Angelotti?

SCARPIA
Angelotti is there?

TOSCA
Sì.

TOSCA
Yes.

SCARPIA *(forte, verso la camera della tortura)*
Basta, Roberti.

SCARPIA *(loudly, towards the torture chamber)*
Enough, Roberti!

SCIARRONE *(che ha aperto l'uscio)*
È svenuto!

SCIARRONE *(re-opening the door)*
He has fainted!

TOSCA *(a Scarpia)*
Assassino!
Voglio vederlo.

TOSCA *(to Scarpia)*
Murderer!
I want to see him.

SCARPIA
Portatelo qui.

SCARPIA
Bring in him here.

Sciarrone re-enters and then Cavaradossi, in a faint, carried by the policemen who lay him or the sofa. Tosca runs up, but on seeing her lover spattered with blood, covers her face in fright and horror. Then ashamed of her show of weakness, she kneels beside Cavaradossi, kissing him and weeping. Sciarrone, Roberti, the judge and the scribe go out at the rear. At a sign from Scarpia, Spoletta and the policemen stay behind.

CAVARADOSSI *(riavendosi)*
Floria!

CAVARADOSSI *(as he comes to)*
Floria!

TOSCA *(coprendolo di baci)*
Amore...

CAVARADOSSI
Sei tu?

TOSCA
Quanto hai penato,
anima mia! Ma il sozzo
birro la pagherà!

CAVARADOSSI
Tosca, hai parlato?

TOSCA
No, amor...

CAVARADOSSI
Davver?

SCARPIA *(forte, a Spoletta)*
Nel pozzo...
Del giardino.
Va, Spoletta.

TOSCA *(covering him with kisses)*
Beloved...

CAVARADOSSI
It is you?

TOSCA
How you have suffered.
Oh my soul! But this foul villain
will pay for it!

CAVARADOSSI
Did you speak?

TOSCA
No, beloved

CAVARADOSSI
Truly not?

SCARPIA *(loudly to Spoletta)*
In the well...
in the garden.
Get him, Spoletta.

Exit Spoletta. Cavaradossi has heard; he rises threateningly towards Tosca, but his strength fails him and he falls back on the sofa, bitterly reproachful as he exclaims:

CAVARADOSSI
Ah! M'hai tradito!

TOSCA *(supplichevole)*
Mario!

CAVARADOSSI

CAVARADOSSI
Ah, you have betrayed me!

TOSCA *(beseeching)*
Mario!

CAVARADOSSI

rejecting her embrace and thrusting her from him

Maledetta!

Accursed woman!

SCIARRONE *(irrompe tutto affannoso)*
Eccellenza, quali nuove!

SCIARRONE *(bursting in, breathless)*
Excellency! Bad news!

SCARPIA *(sorpreso)*
Che vuol dir quell'aria afflitta?

SCARPIA *(taken aback)*
What are you looking so worried about?

SCIARRONE
Un messaggio di sconfitta!

SCIARRONE
It is news of defeat!

SCARPIA
Che sconfitta? Come? Dove?

SCARPIA
How? Where? What defeat?

SCIARRONE
A Marengo.

SCIARRONE
At Marengo.

SCARPIA *(impaziente)*
Tartaruga!

SCARPIA *(impatient)*
Blockhead!

SCIARRONE
Bonaparte è vincitor!

SCIARRONE
Bonaparte has won!

SCARPIA
Melas?

SCARPIA
And Melas?

SCIARRONE
No, Melas è in fuga!

SCIARRONE
No. Melas has fled!

Cavaradossi, having listened to Sciarrone with anxious expectation, now, in sheer enthusiasm, finds the strength to rise threateningly towards Scarpia.

CD 2/Track 8   The bleeding Mario, furious at Tosca's betrayal, blindly launches into this revolutionary diatribe against his torturers.

CAVARADOSSI
Vittoria! Vittoria!
L'alba vindice appar
che fa gli empi tremar!
Libertà sorge,
crollan tirannidi!

TOSCA *(cercando disperatamente di calmarlo)*
Mario, taci! Pietà di me!

CAVARADOSSI
Del sofferto martir
me vedrai qui gioir...
Il tuo cor trema,
o Scarpia carnefice!

CAVARADOSSI
Victory! Victory!
The avenging dawn now rises
to make the wicked tremble!
And liberty returns.
The scourge of tyrants!

TOSCA *(trying desperately to calm him)*
Mario, be still! Have pity on me!

CAVARADOSSI
You see me now rejoice
in my own suffering...
And now your blood runs cold,
hangman, Scarpia!

Tosca clutches Cavaradossi and with a rush of broken words tries to calm him, while Scarpia answers with a sardonic smile.

SCARPIA
Braveggia, urla! T'affretta
a palesarmi il fondo dell'alma ria!
Va, moribondo,
il capestro t'aspetta!
(Grida agli sbirri:)
Portatemelo via!

SCARPIA
Go, shout your boasts! Pour out
the last dregs of your vile soul!
Go, for you die,
the hangman's noose awaits you.
(shouts to the policemen)
Take him away!

Sciarrone and the policemen seize Cavaradossi and drag him towards the door. Tosca makes a supreme effort to hold on to him, but they thrust her brutally aside.

TOSCA
Ah, Mario! Mario! con te...con te...

TOSCA
Mario, with you...

SCARPIA
Voi no!

SCARPIA
Not you!

The door closes and Scarpia and Tosca remain alone.

TOSCA *(con un gemito)*
Salvatelo!

TOSCA *(moaning)*
Save him!

SCARPIA
Io?…Voi!

SCARPIA
I?…You rather!

He goes to the table, notes his supper interrupted midway, and again is calm and smiling.

La povera mia cena fu interrotta.

My poor supper was interrupted.

sees Tosca, dejected and motionless, still at the door.

Così accasciata? Via, mia bella signora,
sedete qui. Volete che cerchiamo
insieme il modo di salvarlo?

So downhearted? Come, my fair lady.
Sit down here. Shall we try to find
together a way to save him?

Tosca bestirs herself and looks at him. Scarpia, still smiling, sits down and motions to her to do the same.

E allor sedete, e favelliamo. E intanto
un sorso. È vin di Spagna.

Well then, sit down, and we shall talk.
And first, a sip of wine. It comes from Spain.

He refills the glass and offers it to Tosca.

Un sorso per rincorarvi.

A sip to hearten you.

TOSCA

TOSCA

still staring at Scarpia, she advances towards the table. She sits resolutely facing him, then asks in a tone of the deepest contempt:

Quanto?

How much?

SCARPIA *(imperturbabile, versandosi da bere)*
Quanto?
(Ride.)

SCARPIA *(imperturbable, as she pours his drink)*
How much?
(laughs)

TOSCA
Il prezzo!

TOSCA
What is your price?

CD 2/Track 9 The upward sweeping theme that introduces this aria is associated with
Scarpia's lust.

SCARPIA
Già, mi dicon venal, ma a donna bella
io non mi vendo a prezzo di moneta.
Se la giurata fede
debbo tradir, ne voglio altra mercede.
Quest'ora io l'attendeva!
Già mi struggea
l'amor della diva!
Ma poc'anzi ti mirai
qual non ti vidi mai!
Quel tuo pianto era lava
ai sensi miei e il tuo sguardo
che odio in me dardeggiava,
mie brame inferociva!
Agil qual leopardo
ti avvinghiasti all'amante;
in quell'istante
t'ho giurata mia!
Mia! Sì, t'avrò!...

SCARPIA
Yes, they say that I am venal, but it is not
for money that I will sell myself
to beautiful women. I want other recompense
if I am to betray my oath of office.
I have waited for this hour.
Already in the past I burned
with passion for the Diva.
But tonight I have beheld you
in a new role I had not seen before.
Those tears of yours were lava
to my senses and that fierce hatred
which your eyes shot at me, only fanned
the fire in my blood.
Supple as a leopard
you enwrapped your lover.
In that instant
I vowed you would be mine!
Mine! Yes. I will have you...

He rises and stretches out his arms towards Tosca. She has listened motionless to his
wanton tirade. Now she leaps up and takes refuge behind the sofa.

TOSCA *(correndo alla finestra)*
Piuttosto giù mi avvento!

TOSCA *(running towards the window)*
I'll jump out first!

SCARPIA *(freddamente)*
In pegno il Mario tuo mi resta!

SCARPIA *(coldly)*
I hold your Mario in pawn!

TOSCA
Ah! miserabile...
L'orribil mercato!

TOSCA
Oh,. wretch...
Oh, ghastly bargain...

It suddenly occurs to her to appeal to the Queen, and she runs to the door.

SCARPIA *(ironico)*
Violenza non ti farò. Sei libera. Va pure,
ma è fallace speranza; la Regina
farebbe grazia ad un cadavere!

SCARPIA *(ironically)*
I do you no violence. Go. You are free.
But your hope is vain: the Queen would
merely grant pardon to a corpse

*Tosca draws back in fright, her eyes fixed or Scarpia. She drops on the sofa. She then
looks away from him with a gesture of supreme contempt.*

Come tu m'odii!

How you detest me!

TOSCA
Ah! Dio!

TOSCA
Ah! God!

SCARPIA *(avvicinandosi)*
Così, così ti voglio!

SCARPIA *(approaching)*
Even so, even so I want you!

TOSCA *(con ribrezzo)*
Non toccarmi, demonio; t'odio, t'odio,
abbietto, vile!

TOSCA *(with loathing)*
Don't touch me, devil! I hate you, hate you!
Fiend, base villain!

flees from him in horror

SCARPIA
Che importa?
Spasimi d'ira e spasimi d'amore!

SCARPIA
What does it matter?
Spasms of wrath or spasms of passion...

TOSCA
Vile!

TOSCA
Foul villain!

SCARPIA
Mia!

SCARPIA
You are mine!

trying to seize her

TOSCA
Vile!

TOSCA
Wretch!

retreats behind the table

SCARPIA *(inseguendola)*
Mia...

SCARPIA *(pursuing her)*
Mine!

TOSCA
Aiuto! Aiuto!

TOSCA
Help! Help!

A distant roll of drums draws slowly near, then fades again into the distance.

SCARPIA
Odi?
È il tamburo. S'avvia; guida la scorta
ultima ai condannati. Il tempo passa!

SCARPIA
Do you hear?
It is the drum that leads the way for the
last march of the condemned. Time passes!

*Tosca listens in terrible dread, and then comes back from the window to lean
exhausted on the sofa.*

Sai quale oscura opra laggiù si compia?
Là si drizza un patibolo. Al tuo Mario,
per tuo voler, non resta che un'ora di vita.

Are you aware of what dark work is done
down there? They raise a gallows. By your
wish, your Mario has but one more hour to
live.

He coldly leans on a corner of the sofa and stares at Tosca.

CD 2/Track 10   In one of the most widely loved arias in all of opera, Tosca recalls her steadfast
faith and asks God why she should be repaid with such sorrow.

TOSCA
Vissi d'arte, vissi d'amore,
non feci mai male ad anima viva!...

TOSCA
I lived for art, I lived for love:
Never did I harm a living creature!...

Con man furtiva	Whatever misfortunes I encountered
quante miserie conobbi, aiutai...	I sought with secret hand to succour...
Sempre con fé sincera,	Ever in pure faith,
la mia preghiera	my prayers rose
ai santi tabernacoli salì.	in the holy chapels.
Sempre con fé sincera	Ever in pure faith,
diedi fiori agli altar.	I brought flowers to the altars.
Nell'ora del dolore perché,	in this hour of pain. Why,
perché Signore, perché	why, oh Lord, why
me ne rimuneri così?...	dost Thou repay me thus?
Diedi gioielli	Jewels I brought
della Madonna al manto,	for the Madonna's mantle,
e diedi il canto agli astri,	and songs for the stars in heaven
al ciel, che ne ridean più belli.	that they shone forth with greater radiance.
Nell'ora del dolore perché,	In this hour of distress. Why,
perché, Signore,	why, oh Lord,
perché me ne rimuneri così?	why dost Thou repay me thus?

kneeling before Scarpia

Vedi,	Look at me, oh, behold!
le man giunte io stendo a te!	With clasped hands I beseech you!
Ecco, vedi, e mercé d'un tuo detto,	And, vanquished, I implore
vinta, aspetto...	the help of your word!

CD 2/Track 11   **(00:54)** The theme of Scarpia's lust continues to punctuate the dialogue.

SCARPIA	**SCARPIA**
Sei troppo bella, Tosca, e troppo amante.	Tosca you are too beautiful and too loving.
Cedo. A misero prezzo;	I yield to you. And at a paltry price;
tu, a me una vita, io a te chieggo	you ask me for a life. I ask of you an
un'istante!	instant.

| **TOSCA** *(alzandosi, con un senso di gran disprezzo)* | **TOSCA** *(rising with great contempt)* |
| Va, va, mi fai ribrezzo! | Go, go, you fill me with loathing! |

a knock at the door

SCARPIA
Chi è la?

SCARPIA
Who's there?

SPOLETTA *(entrando trafelato)*
Eccellenza, l'Angelotti al nostro
giungere si uccise.

SPOLETTA *(enters breathless)*
Excellency, Angelotti
killed himself when we arrived.

SCARPIA
Ebbene, lo si appenda
morto alle forche. E l'altro prigioniero?

SCARPIA
Well, then, have him hanged
dead from the gibbet. The other prisoner?

SPOLETTA
Il Cavalier Cavaradossi?
È tutto pronto, Eccellenza!

SPOLETTA
The Cavalier Cavaradossi?
Everything is ready, Excellency.

TOSCA *(fra sé)*
Dio m'assisti!

TOSCA *(to herself)*
God help me!

SCARPIA *(a Spoletta)*
Aspetta.
(a Tosca)
Ebbene?

SCARPIA *(to Spoletta)*
Wait.
(to Tosca)
Well?

Tosca nods assent She weeps with shame and hides her face. To Spoletta

Odi...

Listen...

TOSCA *(interrompendo subito)*
Ma libero all'istante lo voglio...

TOSCA *(suddenly interrupting)*
But I demand that he be freed this instant...

SCARPIA *(a Tosca)*
Occorre simular. Non posso
far grazia aperta. Bisogna che tutti
abbian per morto il cavalier.

SCARPIA *(to Tosca)*
We must dissemble. I cannot openly
grant pardon to him. All must believe
the Cavalier is dead.

points to Spoletta

Quest'uomo fido provvederà.

TOSCA
Chi mi assicura?

SCARPIA
L'ordin ch'io gli darò voi qui presente.
(a Spoletta)
Spoletta, chiudi.

Spoletta shuts the door and comes back to Scarpia.

Ho mutato d'avviso.
Il prigionier sia fucilato...

Tosca starts with terror.

Attendi...

He fixes on Spoletta a hard, significant glance and Spoletta nods in reply that he has guessed his meaning.

Come facemmo del Conte Palmieri.

SPOLETTA
Un'uccisione...

SCARPIA *(subito con marcata intenzione)*
...Simulata! Come
avvenne del Palmieri! Hai ben compreso?

SPOLETTA
Ho ben compreso.

SCARPIA
Va.

This trusted man of mine will see to it.

TOSCA
How can I be sure?

SCARPIA
By the orders I give him in your presence.
(to Spoletta)
Spoletta, shut the door.

I have changed my mind.
The prisoner shall be shot...

Wait a moment...

As we did with Count Palmieri.

SPOLETTA
An execution...

SCARPIA *(significantly stressing his words)*
...A sham one! As we did
with Palmieri! You understand?

SPOLETTA
I understand.

SCARPIA
Go.

TOSCA	**TOSCA**
Voglio avvertirlo io stessa.	I want to explain to him myself.
SCARPIA	**SCARPIA**
E sia.	As you wish.
(a Spoletta)	*(to Spoletta)*
Le darai passo...	You will let her pass...
Bada, all'ora quarta.	And remember, at four o'clock.
SPOLETTA	**SPOLETTA**
Sì. Come Palmieri.	Yes. Like Palmieri.

Exit Spoletta, Scarpia, near the door, listens to his retreating footsteps, and then his whole behaviour changing, advances towards Tosca flushed with passion.

SCARPIA	**SCARPIA**
Io tenni la promessa...	I have kept my promise.
TOSCA *(arrestandolo)*	**TOSCA** *(stopping him)*
Non ancora.	Not yet.
Voglio un salvacondotto onde fuggire	I want a safe conduct, so that he and I
dallo Stato con lui.	can flee the State together.
SCARPIA *(con galanteria)*	**SCARPIA** *(gallantly)*
Partir dunque volete?	You want to leave?
TOSCA	**TOSCA**
Sì, per sempre!	Yes, for ever.

CD 2/Track 12   As Scarpia writes up the necessary papers for the lovers' escape, we hear a theme in the orchestra associated with Tosca's distress. As he approaches to embrace her, **(01:51)** we again hear the "lust" motive.

SCARPIA	**SCARPIA**
Si adempia il voler vostro.	Your wish shall be granted.

He goes to the desk and begins writing. He stops to ask:

E qual via scegliete?

And which road do you prefer?

As he writes, Tosca goes up to the table to take, with shaking hand, the glass of wine that Scarpia has poured, but as she lifts it to her lips, her eye falls on a sharply pointed knife that is lying on the table. She sees that Scarpia at this moment is absorbed in writing, and so, with infinite caution, still answering his questions, and never taking her eye from him, she reaches out for the knife.

TOSCA
La più breve!

TOSCA
The shortest!

SCARPIA
Civitavecchia?

SCARPIA
Civitavecchia?

TOSCA
Sì.

TOSCA
Yes.

Finally, she is able to grasp the knife. Still watching Scarpia, she hides it behind her as she leans against the table. He has now finished making out the pass. He puts his seal upon it and folds the paper, and then, opening his arms, advances towards Tosca to embrace her.

SCARPIA
Tosca, finalmente mia!

SCARPIA
Tosca, now you are mine at last!

But his shout of lust ends in a cry of anguish: Tosca has struck him full in the breast.

Maledetta!

Accursed one!

TOSCA
Questo è il bacio di Tosca!

TOSCA
This is the kiss of Tosca!

Scarpia stretches out an arm towards her, swaying and lurching as he advances, seeking her aid. She eludes him, but is suddenly caught between him and the table, and seeing that he is about to touch her, she thrusts him back in horror. Scarpia crashes to the floor, shrieking in a voice nearly stifled with blood.

SCARPIA
Aiuto...muoio! Soccorso! Muoio!

SCARPIA
Help! I am dying! Help! I die!

Tosca

Tosca

watches him as he struggles helplessly on the floor and clutches at the sofa, trying to pull himself up

Ti soffoca il sangue?	Is your blood choking you?
E ucciso da una donna!	And killed by a woman!
M'hai assai torturata?	Did you torment me enough?
Odi tu ancora? Parla!	Can you still hear me? Speak!
Guardami! Son Tosca! O Scarpia!	Look at me! I am Tosca! Oh, Scarpia!

Scarpia

Scarpia

after a last effort he falls back

Soccorso! Aiuto!	Help! Help!

Tosca (*chinandosi verso Scarpia*)	**Tosca** (*bending over him*)
Ti soffoca il sangue?	Is your blood choking you?
Muori dannato! Muori! Muori! Muori!	Die accursed! Die! Die! Die!

seeing him motionless

È morto! Or gli perdono!	He is dead! And now I pardon him!
E avanti a lui tremava tutta Roma!	All Rome trembled before him!

Her eyes still fixed or the body, Tosca goes to the table, puts down the knife, takes a bottle of water, wets a napkin and washes her fingers. She then goes to the mirror to arrange her hair Then she hunts for the safe-conduct pass on the desk, and not finding it there she turns and sees the paper in the clenched hand of the dead man. She takes it with a shudder and hides it in her bosom. She puts out the candle on the table and is about to leave when a scruple detains her. She returns to the desk and takes the candle there, using it to relight the other, and then places one to the right and the other to the left of Scarpia's head. She rises and looks about her and notices a crucifix on the wall. She removes it with reverent care, and returning to the dead man, kneels at his side and places it on his breast. She rises, approaches the door cautiously, goes out and closes it.

Act 3

The platform of Castel Sant'Angelo

(At left, a casemate: there is a lamp, large registry book with writing materials, a bench and a chair. A crucifix hangs or one of the casemate walls with a lamp in front. To the right, the door to a small stairway leading up to the platform. In the distance, the Vatican and the Basilica of St Peter's. It is still night, but gradually darkness is dispelled by the grey, uncertain light of the hour before dawn. Church bells toll for matins. The voice of a shepherd passing with his flock can be heard.)

CD 2/Track 13 Act III begins with a triumphant horn call which the lovers' will sing again in their short-lived assurance that all will be well. This gives way to the curious shepherd's tune (01:33), written on an ancient poem with the melody written in the ancient lydian mode. (02:35) As dawn breaks, we hear church bells from varying distances, accompanied by a tender reflective motive in the strings derived from fragments of many themes heard in the opera. **(05:28)** Cavaradossi is led to his cell by the soldiers, and the orchestra plays the regretful theme of his upcoming aria.

VOCE DEL PASTORE	VOICE OF SHEPHERD
Io de' sospiri.	I give you sighs,
Ve ne rimanno tanti	there are as many
pe' quante foje	as there are leaves
ne smoveno li venti.	driven by the wind.
Tu me disprezzi. Io mi ciaccoro.	You may scorn me, and my heart is sick.
Lampena d'oro, me fai morir.	Oh lamp of gold, I die for you.

A jailer with a lantern mounts the stairs from below. He goes to the casemate and lights the light in front of the crucifix, and then the one or the table. He sits down and waits, half drowsing. Soon a picket of guards, led by a sergeant, emerges from the stairway with Cavaradossi. The picket halts as the sergeant leads Cavaradossi to the casemate and hands a note to the jailer. The latter examines it, opens the registry book and writes, as he questions the prisoner.

CARCERIERE
Mario Cavaradossi?

JAILER
Mario Cavaradossi?

Cavaradossi bows his head in acknowledgement. The jailer hands the pen to the sergeant.

A voi.
(a Cavaradossi)
Vi resta un'ora;
un sacerdote i vostri cenni attende.

For you.
(to Cavaradossi)
You have one hour.
A priest awaits your call.

CAVARADOSSI
No, ma un'ultima grazia io vi richiedo.

CAVARADOSSI
No...but I have a last favour to ask of you.

CARCERIERE
Se posso...

JAILER
If I can...

CAVARADOSSI
Io lascio al mondo
una persona cara. Consentite
ch'io le scriva un sol motto.

CAVARADOSSI
One very dear person
I leave behind me. Permit me
to write her a few lines.

taking a ring from his finger

Unico resto
di mia ricchezza è questo anel.
Se promettete di consegnarle
il mio ultimo addio,
esso è vostro.

This ring is all that remains
of my possessions.
If you will promise to give her
my last farewell,
then it is yours.

CARCERIERE

JAILER

hesitates a little, then accepts. He motions Cavaradossi to the chair at the table, and sits down on the bench.

Scrivete.

Write.

CD 2/Track 15 In one of the most famous arias in the tenor repertoire, "E lucevan le stelle," Mario reflects on the world he leaves behind. Puccini fought with his librettists about the appropriate tone for this aria, and in the end wrote much of the poetry for it himself. It is, in a word, perfect.

CAVARADOSSI

CAVARADOSSI

begins to write, but after a few lines a flood of memories invades him

E lucevan le stelle ed olezzava	And the stars shone and the earth was perfumed.
la terra, stridea l'uscio	The gate to the garden creaked
dell'orto, e un passo sfiorava la rena...	and a footstep rustled the sand to the path...
Entrava ella, fragrante,	Fragrant. she entered
mi cadea fra le braccia...	and fell into my arms...
Oh, dolci baci, o languide carezze,	Oh soft kisses, oh sweet abandon,
mentr'io fremente	as I trembling
le belle forme disciogliea dai veli!	unloosed her veils and disclosed her beauty.
Svanì per sempre il sogno mio d'amore...	Oh vanished forever is that dream of love,
L'ora è fuggita...	fled is that hour,
E muoio disperato!	and desperately I die.
E non ho amato mai tanto la vita!	And never before have I loved so much!

He bursts into sobs, Spoletta appears at the stairhead, The sergeant at his side and Tosca following. Spoletta indicates where Cavaradossi is and then calls the jailer. He warns the guard at the rear to keep careful watch on the prisoner, and then leaves with the sergeant and the jailer. Tosca sees Cavaradossi weeping his head in his arms. She lifts his head, and he jumps to his feet in astonishment. Tosca shows him a note but is far too overcome with emotion to speak.

CD 2/Track 16 Tosca's theme begins softly in the orchestra and builds to a breathtaking climax as she enters to greet Mario with the news of Scarpia's murder and their imminent freedom. She tells him the story of the villain's death accompanied by a collage of themes from the second act.

(leggendo)
Ah! Franchigia a Floria Tosca...
...e al cavalier che l'accompagna.

TOSCA

reading with him in a hoarse and shaken voice

...e al cavalier che l'accompagna.
(a Cavaradossi con un grido d'esultanza)
Sei libero!

CAVARADOSSI *(guarda il foglio; ne vede la firma)*
Scarpia!...
Scarpia che cede? La prima
sua grazia è questa...

TOSCA
E l'ultima!

CAVARADOSSI
Che dici?

TOSCA
Il tuo sangue o il mio amore
volea. Fur vani scongiuri e pianti.
Invan, pazza d'orror,
alla Madonna mi volsi e ai Santi...
l'empio mostro dicea:
già nei cieli
il patibol le braccia leva!
Rullavano i tamburi...
Rideva, l'empio mostro, rideva,
già la sua preda pronto a ghermir!
"Sei mia?" Sì. Alla sua brama
mi promisi. Lì presso
luccicava una lama...

(reading)
Ah! A safe-conduct for Floria Tosca...
...and for the Cavalier accompanying her.

TOSCA

...and for the Cavalier accompanying her.
(to Cavaradossi with an exultant cry)
You are free!

CAVARADOSSI *(studies the pass and sees the signature)*
Scarpia! Scarpia yields? This is the first
act of clemency...

TOSCA
And his last!

CAVARADOSSI
What?

TOSCA
Either your blood or my love he demanded: my entreaties and my tears were useless.
Wild with horror, I appealed in vain
to the Madonna and the Saints.
The damnable monster told me
that already the gallows
stretched their arms skyward!
The drums rolled and
he laughed, the evil monster, laughed,
ready to spring and carry off his prey!
Is it yes? He asked, and yes, I promised
myself to his lust. But there at hand
a sharp blade glittered:

Ei scrisse il foglio liberator,
venne all'orrendo amplesso...
Io quella lama gli piantai nel cor.

CAVARADOSSI
Tu, di tua man l'uccidesti?
Tu pia, tu benigna, e per me!

TOSCA
N'ebbi le mani tutte lorde di sangue!

CAVARADOSSI

lovingly taking her hands in his

O dolci mani mansuete e pure,
o mani elette a bell'opre pietose,
a carezzar fanciulli, a coglier rose,
a pregar, giunte, per le sventure,
dunque in voi, fatte dall'amor secure,
giustizia le sue sacre armi depose?
Voi deste morte, o mani vittoriose,
o dolci mani mansuete e pure!

TOSCA

disengaging her hands from his

Senti, l'ora è vicina. Io già raccolsi
oro e gioielli, una vettura è pronta...

Ma prima...ridi amor...prima sarai fucilato...
per finta, ad armi scariche.
Simulato supplizio. Al colpo, cadi;
i soldati sen vanno, e noi siam salvi!
Poscia a Civitavecchia, una tartana,
e via per mar!

he wrote out the liberating pass,
and came to claim the horrible embrace –
That pointed blade I planted in his heart.

CAVARADOSSI
You, with your own hand you killed him?
You tender, you gentle – and for me

TOSCA
My hands were reeking with his blood!

CAVARADOSSI

Oh sweet hands pure and gentle.
Oh hands meant for the fair works of piety,
caressing children, gathering roses,
for prayers when others meet misfortune...
Then it was in you, made strong by love,
that justice placed her sacred weapons?
You dealt out death, victorious hands,
oh sweet hand pure and gentle.

TOSCA

Listen the hour is near. I have already
collected my gold and jewels. A carriage is
waiting...
But first...Oh, laugh at this my love...
First you will be shot, in play and pretence,
with unloaded arms...mock punishment.
Fall down at the shot, The soldiers leave,
and we are safe! And then to Civitavecchia,
and there a ship. And we're away by sea!

CAVARADOSSI
Liberi!

TOSCA
Liberi!

CAVARADOSSI
Via pel mar!

TOSCA
Chi si duole in terra più?
Senti effluvi di rose?
Non ti par che le cose
aspettan tutte innamorate il sole?

CAVARADOSSI *(con la più tenera commozione)*
Amaro sol per te m'era il morire,
da te la vita prende ogni splendore,
all'esser mio la gioia ed il desire
nascon di te, come di fiamma ardore.
Io folgorare i cieli e scolorire

vedrò nell'occhio tuo rivelatore,
e la beltà delle cose più mire
avrà sol da te voce e colore.

TOSCA
Amor che seppe a te vita serbare
ci sarà guida in terra, e in mar nocchiere,
e vago farà il mondo riguardare,
finché congiunti alle celesti sfere
dileguerem, siccome alte sul mare
al sol cadente, nuvole leggere!

CAVARADOSSI
Free!

TOSCA
Free!

CAVARADOSSI
Away by sea!

TOSCA
Where now have pain and sorrow fled?
Do you smell the aroma of the roses?
Do you feel that all things on the earth
await the sun enamoured?

CAVARADOSSI *(with tender exaltation)*
Only for you did death taste bitter for me,
and only you invest this life with splendour.
All joy and all desire. for my being,
are held in you as heat within flame.
I now shall see through your transfiguring eyes,
The heavens blaze and the heavens darken;
and the beauty of all things remarkable from
you alone will have their voice and colour.

TOSCA
The love that found the way to save your life
shall be our guide on earth,
our pilot on the waters,
and make the wide world lovely to our eyes;
until together we shall fade away
beyond the sphere of earth, as light clouds
fade, at sundown, high above the sea.

They are stirred and silent. Then Tosca recalled to reality, looks about uneasily.

As Tosca instructs Mario on how to act convincingly in his "mock" execution, the orchestra's mood is almost giddy. This delightful theme is derived from her first-act aria describing their love nest. Convinced that all is well, they join in an a capella strain, **(01:06)** first heard in the horns at the beginning of the act.

E non giungono...

They still! don't come...

turning to Cavaradossi with affectionate concern

Bada!
Al colpo egli è mestiere
che tu subito cada...

And be careful!
When you hear the shot
you must fall down at once...

CAVARADOSSI *(la rassicura)*
Non temere
che cadrò sul momento, e al naturale.

CAVARADOSSI *(reassuring her)*
Have no fear,
I'll fall on the instant, and quite naturally.

TOSCA *(insistente)*
Ma stammi attento di non farti male!
Con scenica scienza
io saprei la movenza.

TOSCA *(insisting)*
But be careful not to hurt yourself.
With my experience in the theatre
I should know how to manage it.

CAVARADOSSI
(la interrompe, attirandola a sé)
Parlami ancora come dianzi parlavi,
è così dolce il suon della tua voce!

CAVARADOSSI
(interrupting and drawing her to him)
Speak to me again as you spoke before.
So sweet is the sound of your voice.

TOSCA *(si abbandona, quasi estasiata)*
Uniti ed esulanti
diffonderan pel mondo i nostri amori,
armonie di colori...

TOSCA *(carried away with rapture)*
Together in exile
we shall bear our love through the world.
Harmonies of colour...

TOSCA E CAVARADOSSI
Armonie di canti diffonderem!
(con grande entusiasmo)
Trionfal...
Di nova speme

TOSCA AND CAVARADOSSI
And harmonies of song!
(ecstatically)
Triumphant...
The soul trembles

l'anima freme
in celestial
crescente ardor.
Ed in armonico vol
già l'anima va
all'estasi d'amor.

TOSCA
Gli occhi ti chiuderò con mille baci
e mille ti dirò nomi d'amor.

with new hope
in heavenly
increasing ardour.
And in harmonious flight
the spirit soars
to the ecstasy of love.

TOSCA
With a thousand kisses I shall seal your eyes.
And call you by a thousand names of love.

Meanwhile a squad of soldiers has entered from the stairway. The officer in command ranges them to the rear. Enter Spoletta, the sergeant and the jailer, Spoletta giving the necessary orders. The sky lightens; dawn appears; a bell strikes four. The jailer goes to Cavaradossi, removes his cap and nods towards the officer.

CARCERIERE
L'ora!

JAILER
It is time.

CAVARADOSSI
Son pronto.

CAVARADOSSI
I am ready.

The jailer takes the registry of the condemned and leaves by the stairway.

TOSCA *(a Cavaradossi, con voce bassissima e ridendo di soppiatto)*
Tieni a mente: al primo colpo, giù...

TOSCA *(to Cavaradossi, speaking low and laughing secretly)*
Remember: at the first shot, down...

CAVARADOSSI *(sottovoce, ridendo esso pure)*
Giù...

CAVARADOSSI *(in a low voice. also laughing)*
Down...

TOSCA
Né rialzarti innanzi ch'io ti chiami.

TOSCA
And don't get up before I call you...

CAVARADOSSI
No, amor!

CAVARADOSSI
No, beloved!

Tosca E cadi bene.	**Tosca** And fall down properly…
Cavaradossi Come la Tosca in teatro.	**Cavaradossi** Like Tosca on the stage…
Tosca Non ridere…	**Tosca** You mustn't laugh…
Cavaradossi Così?	**Cavaradossi** So?
Tosca Così.	**Tosca** So.

Their farewells over, Cavaradossi follows the officer. Tosca takes her place on the left side of the casemate, in position, however, to observe what is happening on the platform. She sees the officer and the sergeant lead Cavaradossi towards the wall directly facing her. The sergeant wishes to blindfold Cavaradossi who declines with a smile. The grim preparations begin to strain Tosca's patience.

CD 2/Track 19   The theme of the execution begins softly in the orchestra and slowly builds until the firing squad's rifles are heard. Mario falls, and the full orchestra reiterates the theme **(01:28)**, this time with a wild, unreal quality reflecting Tosca's relief sense of relief against the backdrop of Mario's all-too-real death.

Tosca Com'è lunga l'attesa! Perché indugiano ancor? Già sorge il sole; perché indugiano ancora? È una commedia, lo so, ma questa angoscia eterna pare.	**Tosca** How long is this waiting! Why are they still! delaying? The sun already rises. Why are they still! delaying? It is only a comedy, I know, but this anguish seems to last for ever!

The officer and the sergeant marshal the squad of soldiers before the wall and impart their instructions.

Ecco! Apprestano l'armi! Com'è bello
il mio Mario!

There! They are taking aim! How handsome
my Mario is!

The officer lowers his sabre, the platoon fires and Cavaradossi falls.

Là! Muori! Ecco un artista!

There! Die! Ah, what an actor!

*The sergeant goes up to examine the fallen man. Spoletta also approaches to prevent
the sergeant from delivering the coup de grace, and he covers Cavaradossi with a
cloak. The officer realigns the soldiers. The sergeant withdraws the sentinel from his
post at the rear and Spoletta leads the group off by the stairway. Tosca follows this
scene with the utmost agitation, fearing that Cavaradossi may lose patience and
move or speak before the proper moment. In a hushed voice she warns him:*

O Mario, non ti muovere...
S'avviano, taci! Vanno, scendono.

Oh Mario, do not move...
They're going now. Be still. They are going
down...

*Seeing the platform deserted, she goes to listen at the stairhead. She stands there for
a moment in breathless dread as she thinks she hears the soldiers returning. Again
in a low voice she warns Cavaradossi:*

Ancora non ti muovere...

Not yet, you mustn't move...

She listens: they have all gone. She runs towards Cavaradossi.

Presto! Su, Mario! Mario! Su! Presto!
Andiam! Su! Su!

Quickly! Up, Mario! Mario! Up! Quickly.
Come. Up! Up!

She kneels and quickly removes the cloak and leaps to her feet pale and terrified.

Mario! Mario! Morto! Morto!

Mario! Mario! Dead! Dead!

sobbing she throws herself on Cavaradossi's body

O Mario, morto? Tu? Così? Finire così?
Così! ecc.

Oh Mario, dead? You? Like this? Dead like
this? etc.

From the courtyard below the parapet and from the narrow stairway come the confused voices of Spoletta, Sciarrone and the soldiers. They draw nearer.

VOCI CONFUSE
Scarpia? Pugnalato!
La donna è Tosca!
Che non sfugga!

CONFUSED VOICES
Scarpia stabbed?
The woman is Tosca!
Don't let her escape.

Spoletta rushes in from the stairway, and behind him Sciarrone shouting and waving at Tosca.

SCIARRONE
È lei!

SCIARRONE
There she is!

SPOLETTA *(gettandosi su Tosca)*
Ah, Tosca, pagherai
ben cara la sua vita!

SPOLETTA *(charging towards Tosca)*
Ah, Tosca you will pay
for his life most dearly!

Tosca springs to her feet, pushing Spoletta violently, answering:

TOSCA
Colla mia!

TOSCA
With my own!

Spoletta falls back from the sudden thrust. Tosca escapes and runs to the parapet, she leaps onto it and hurls herself over the ledge, crying:

O Scarpia, avanti a Dio!

Oh Scarpia! Before God!

Sciarrone and soldiers rush in confusion to the parapet and look down. Spoletta stands stunned and pale.

CD 2/Track 20

(00:56) Tosca hurls herself off the parapet as the nostalgic theme of Mario's farewell to the world soars in the orchestra, and the opera comes to its tragic close.

END

Tosca

GIACOMO PUCCINI 1858–1924
LIBRETTO BY GIUSEPPE GIACOSA & LUIGI ILLICA AFTER VICTORIEN SARDOU

OPERA IN THREE ACTS

Floria Tosca	RENATA SCOTTO
Mario Cavaradossi	PLACIDO DOMINGO
Scarpia	RENATO BRUSON
Cesare Angelotti	JOHN CHEEK
Spoletta	ANDREA VELIS
Un sagrestano	RENATO CAPECCHI
Sciarrone	PAUL HUDSON
Un carceriere	ITZHAK PERLMAN
Un pastore	DOMINICK MARTINEZ

Ambrosian Opera Chorus
Chorus Master: John McCarthy

St Clement Danes School Boys' Choir
Trained by: Keith Walters

Philharmonia Orchestra
Conducted by   James Levine

Répétiteur: Roger Vignoles
Language coaches: Ubaldo Gardini & Gwyn Morris
Children's coach: Jean Povey

COMPACT DISC 1 46.08

COMPACT DISC 2 70.11

Atto Terzo/Act Three/Dritter Akt/Troisième Acte